MW01089025

LADY GAGA
IS LIFE

A Superfan's Guide to
All Things We Love about Lady Gaga

KATHLEEN PERRICONE

ILLUSTRATED BY NATALIA SANABRIA

CONTENTS

INTRODUCTION

Lady Gaga is "talented, brilliant, incredible, amazing, showstopping, spectacular, never the same, totally unique . . ." The embodiment of pop art, she has revolutionized both pop music and pop culture: Gaga is the first female artist to have four singles sell at least ten million copies ("Just Dance," "Poker Face," "Bad Romance," and "Shallow")—and the only one to do it while wearing meat, bubbles, a pyrotechnic bra, half-smoked cigarette sunglasses, and Alexander McQueen twelve-inch (30 cm) Armadillo heels. The double threat has also made her mark on Hollywood, beginning with her Academy Award—nominated debut in 2018's *A Star Is Born* opposite Bradley Cooper.

A decade earlier, the avant-garde New Yorker launched into overnight superstardom with her first album, *The Fame*, which, along with its 2009 reissue *The Fame Monster*, sold eighteen million copies and won five Grammy Awards. (As of 2023, *The Fame* remains the twelfth-biggest album of all time on the *Billboard* 200 chart). Gaga's second album, *Born This Way*, spawned an anthem of the same name, which became the fastest-selling song on iTunes in 2011, with a

HERS HAS BEEN
AN ENTERTAINMENT CAREER
MOST COULD ONLY DREAM OF.

million downloads in five days. "Applause," the lead single off 2013's *Artpop*, charted in nearly two dozen countries around the world.

Mother Monster is also the mother of reinvention: In 2016, she stripped away the theatrics for the soft rock–Americana *Joanne* and partnered with the one and only Tony Bennett on two Grammy-winning jazz albums, *Cheek to Cheek* (2014) and *Love for Sale* (2021). Proving her versatility as an artist, she jumped right back into Gaga mode for 2020's *Chromatica*, which gifted pop music fans an iconic collaboration with Ariana Grande, "Rain on

Me." The following year, she ushered in a new chapter for America when she performed the national anthem at President Joe Biden's inauguration—in bulletproof haute couture, no less.

Growing up in New York City, Gaga (born Stefani Germanotta) got her start in school productions of *Guys and Dolls* and *A Funny Thing Happened on the Way to the Forum*. She returned to acting, her first love, as the star of *American Horror Story: Hotel* in 2015, and then got to combine her two skills in *A Star Is Born*, which gave the world one of the best-selling soundtracks of all time, and the 2024 musical sequel *Joker: Folie à Deux*.

Hers has been an entertainment career most could only dream of, filled with Little Monsters, paparazzi, six world tours, the Super Bowl, the Oscars, thirteen Grammys, more than thirty music videos, and plenty of references to Gaga's pop-art idol, Andy Warhol. Over a decade ago, in her first cover story for *Rolling Stone* in 2009, Gaga revealed the path ahead: "I feel like I have so much to do. The whole world sees the number-one records and the rise in sales and recognition, but my true legacy will be the test of time, and whether I can sustain a space in pop culture and really make stuff that will have a genuine impact."

PART ONE

Born This Way

NEW YORK DOLL

For a prodigy of music and the arts, New York City offered inspiration at every turn. Lady Gaga (born Stefani Joanne Angelina Germanotta) grew up on the Upper West Side just a few blocks north of Lincoln Center, home to the New York City Ballet and Metropolitan Opera. Her school was a stone's throw from the Guggenheim's permanent collection of Picasso, Van Gogh, O'Keeffe, and Pollock. And on the walk home to the Germanotta duplex on West 70th Street, she could cut through Central Park and stop to visit the John Lennon memorial, which she did several times a week.

In 1990, when she was just four, Gaga first took interest in the family's piano. The toddler was too short to see the keys, but she could reach them, and she would tickle the ivories to the tune of her own invented songs. Noticing their daughter's natural talent, Joe and Cynthia Germanotta enrolled her in lessons. Her first teacher also stoked her interest in fashion, as the little girl became obsessed with her long nails. "I didn't know this at the time, but she was actually a stripper," Gaga revealed in the 2011 MTV special *Inside the Outside*. Another teacher attempted to tone down the prodigy's theatrical playing style. To make her hands less "floppy," she tied a string around Gaga's wrists and hung a Pink Panther action figure between them, so when she practiced scales up and down the piano, she had to play evenly to balance the toy.

The first CD Gaga bought with her own money was Green Day's *Dookie* (1994), a modern addition to a classic music collection crafted by her parents that included the Beatles, Stevie Wonder, Elton John, Bruce Springsteen, and Pink Floyd. Joe imparted his love of rock and roll to his daughter, who only knew how to play classical pieces by Beethoven, Mozart, Bach, and Chopin. One Christmas, she received a Springsteen songbook with "Thunder Road" from Joe, who made her a deal: "If you learn how to play this song, we will take out a loan for a baby grand piano."

The Germanottas were middle-class, with all the money Joe earned from running a Wi-Fi installation company and Cynthia's telecommunications salary going toward the mortgage and their children's educations. Gaga and her younger sister, Natali, attended Convent of the Sacred Heart, an all-girls Catholic school where annual tuition was upward of $50,000 per student. On Saturdays, Gaga attended a full day of acting classes, and in the summers, creative arts camp.

"'THESE WERE THE WORDS THAT CHANGED MY LIFE. HE LOOKED AT ME AND SAID, 'HAVE YOU EVER THOUGHT ABOUT WRITING MUSIC?'"'

At thirteen, she began taking voice lessons from Don Lawrence, who had worked with Mick Jagger, Bono, and teen pop star Christina Aguilera. His nephew overheard Gaga singing to herself as she shopped at an Upper East Side fashion boutique and put the two in contact. Lawrence immediately recognized that she understood musical scales from her years as a pianist and encouraged Gaga to combine her talents. "These were the words that changed my life," she recalled in the MTV special. "He looked at me and said, 'Have you ever thought about writing music? . . . I think you would be good at writing songs.'" Three weeks later, she penned her first, a power ballad called "To Love Again."

Gaga also had a passion for musical theater, and in high school she scored the lead in *Guys and Dolls*. It was the greatest moment of her life (to that point)—and her father threatened to take it away as punishment for bad behavior. The teen had a twentysomething boyfriend and was sneaking out at night to party downtown with a fake ID. When Joe cut off her allowance, she got a waitressing job at a diner to fund her rebellious adventures. She also used her earnings for her first big purchase, a Gucci bag (two decades before she starred in 2021's *House of Gucci*).

At school, the only rule the straight-A student broke pertained to the strict dress code, which called for knee-length skirts and prohibited makeup or nail polish. "I would wear shirts that were low-cut," said Gaga, who earned the nickname Big Boobs McGee. Her last name inspired another: The Germ, coined by classmates who were jealous of her artistic opportunities. In addition to school plays, she was cast in a 2001 episode of HBO's *The Sopranos*, as a chain-smoking bad girl who corrupts Tony's son. Meanwhile, Gaga was also pursuing her musical dreams: She started a classic rock cover band, performed at open mic nights at the Songwriters Hall of Fame, and even cut a demo of original songs, which she gave out as party favors at her Sweet Sixteen. Everyone who heard it thought, "Whoa, she's going to be a star," friend Justin Rodriguez told *New York Magazine*. "She was by far the most talented person in high school."

But how would she rank in college? At seventeen, Gaga gained early admission to New York University's musical theater training conservatory, Collaborative Arts Project 21, which only admits sixty students every year. In the fall of 2003, she left the Upper West Side for the Greenwich Village campus three miles away. Once again, her talent and determination rubbed some the wrong way. Former classmate Carly Waddell, best known as a contestant on *The Bachelor*, revealed in 2023 that during lunch breaks at NYU "[Gaga] would sit at the piano every single day and just play and sing *Wicked* at the top of her lungs . . . Was she good? Of course! She was great, but I just wanted to eat my sandwich."

Gaga later confessed that she did feel creatively out of place at NYU, which is why she dropped out after three semesters. "I thought I could teach myself about art better than the school could," she told *Elle* in 2013. "I really felt New York was my teacher and that I needed to bite the bullet and go it alone. I wasn't interested in going to frat parties and doing those sorts of collegiate things. I was really interested in the music scene and waitressing and cleaning toilets, or whatever the fuck it was I was doing." Her parents disapproved, but they agreed she could take a year off to figure it out. If she was not successful, she would have to return to NYU.

The nineteen-year-old found her own apartment on the Lower East Side, the complete opposite of the Upper West Side—and exactly the change of scenery she needed. "When I grew up by Lincoln Center, I wasn't able to access all of the things that were on the Lower East Side, and I wasn't in a school that was enriching culturally in that way," Gaga described in *Inside the Outside*. "It was like I needed to fuck myself up and go underground for a couple years to understand New York City and understand a whole different side of the pavement . . . I wanted to get deeper into New York."

MOST LIKELY TO BECOME FAMOUS

Lady Gaga isn't the only notable graduate of Convent of the Sacred Heart. The all-girls school has educated Kennedys, Vanderbilts . . . and Hiltons. Hotel-heiresses-turned-reality-stars Paris and Nicki Hilton attended the K–12 institution at the same time as Gaga, although the three students were several grades apart and ran in different circles. Paris, the eldest, was a junior in high school when eleven-year-old Gaga started at Sacred Heart, and later transferred to a different school, but her younger sister stayed and graduated two years ahead of Gaga.

"I didn't hang out with all the popular blonde girls," the natural brunette confessed to the *Daily Star*. But she did remember the wealthy sisters as "very pretty and very clean." Gaga and Paris didn't actually meet until 2009, when the heiress interviewed Gaga backstage at a Nokia party in London. "You've become an icon . . . I'm loving your music," gushed Paris, who had a Top 20 hit of her own with "Stars Are Blind." "I'd love to do a song with you." The two have yet to collaborate, but Paris remains in awe. She's publicly raved over "my fellow Sacred Heart alum"—even on her honeymoon in 2022, while watching Gaga's film *House of Gucci*.

LADY IS A VAMP

Three years before Stefani reinvented herself as Lady Gaga, she was recast as a downtown bohemian: She dyed her blonde-highlighted hair jet black and straightened her curls, hung a Yoko Ono record over her bed, and read poetry. The college dropout started a band with three guys she knew from NYU dubbed the Stefani Germanotta Band, or SGBand for short, and they built up a small following around Lower Manhattan. Their live shows included a mix of originals and classic rock covers, with the talented teen taking center stage with her keyboard.

For their first gig in December 2005, at the Lion's Den in Greenwich Village, Gaga wore "a big white hippie skirt" and a green tube top with a flower in her hair. For ninety minutes, "We played a bunch of songs nobody knew," she recalled with a laugh on MTV's *Inside the Outside*. "I was so delusional."

But she was developing quite a fan base. With the SGBand—Calvin Pia (guitar), Eli Silverman (bass), and Alex Beckham (percussion)—she recorded two five-song EPs, *Word* and *red and bleu*, and the CDs sold out at every local gig. Among the crowd favorites was "Hollywood" and the Hurricane Katrina—inspired "No Floods," which Gaga performed live on NBC at the 2005 Columbus Day Parade in New York City. "She's only nineteen and what a voice," anchor Maria Bartiromo remarked on the broadcast. Six months later, in March 2006, the SGBand leader got her biggest opportunity to date as one of the nine rising stars selected for the Songwriters Hall of Fame's New Songwriters Showcase. Introduced by HOF director Bob Leone as "a tiny person with a big voice and a lot of love to spread," she was welcomed to the stage with cheers and whistles.

One of the people in the audience that night at the Cutting Room was Wendy Starland, a singer-songwriter who had been tasked by her New Jersey—based producer Rob Fusari with helping him find a female singer who had the look to "front a band like the Strokes" but, more importantly, a dynamic stage presence. As Starland watched the five-foot-two brunette rock the tiny stage, she knew this was that girl.

"Stefani's confidence filled the room," Starland recalled to *New York Magazine*. "Her presence is enormous. And fearless. I listened for the pitch, the tone, and timbre of her voice. Was she able to have a huge dynamic range? Was she able to get soft and then belt? And I felt that she was able to do all that while giving out this very powerful energy." Starland rushed outside the venue to call Fusari, who didn't appreciate being woken up at such a late hour. But it was worth it, she promised. "I said I found the girl. 'What? It's really one in a million. What's her name?' Stefani Germanotta. 'Um, you gotta be kidding me,'" he groused.

Fusari, whose musical résumé included three Destiny's Child albums and Will Smith's 1999 smash, "Wild Wild West," was perplexed by his new protégé. He immediately realized she was not what he *thought* he was looking for, a female Julian Casablancas. "I thought she was a female John Lennon, to be totally honest," he confessed to *New York Magazine*. "She was the oddest talent." Playing to her strengths, they developed piano-driven songs influenced by classic rock bands Led Zeppelin, Jefferson Airplane, and Queen—and it was Freddie Mercury's "Radio Ga Ga" that inspired Stefani's new moniker, Lady Gaga. Seven days a week, the twenty-year-old would wake up early to catch the bus out of New York's Port Authority to Fusari's home studio an hour away in Parsippany. Everything was hanging on this opportunity: Joe Germanotta's one-year deadline for his daughter to make something happen or go back to college had arrived.

Lady Gaga and Fusari shifted the focus of their songwriting from rock to pop-driven dance and cranked out songs like "Paparazzi" and "Beautiful, Dirty, Rich" that would appear on her 2008 debut album, *The Fame*. In the fall of 2006, the buzz about the piano-playing powerhouse reached Island Def Jam, and the record label invited her to its Times Square office for a meeting with L.A. Reid, the man credited with shaping the music careers of Rihanna, Justin Bieber, Pink, and Usher. He signed Lady Gaga to a deal worth $850,000—but after she turned in three finished songs, he changed his mind. According to her representative at the label, Reid didn't even make it through one track before looking up and making a cutthroat gesture. Lady Gaga had been dropped.

"I went back to my apartment on the Lower East Side, and I was so depressed," she confessed to *New York Magazine*. "That's when I started the real devotion to my music and art."

She found her creative equal in the similarly named Lady Starlight, a thirtysomething performance artist who shared Gaga's love of heavy metal, fashion, and bad boys. The two crossed paths at St. Jerome's, a dive bar on the Lower East Side where Gaga go-go danced on the bar to make ends meet, earning as much as $400 a night in cash. Together, they formed Lady Gaga and the Starlight Revue, a pop-metal burlesque show that lit up the downtown scene, literally—their go-to gag was to set hairspray on fire. Gaga and Starlight quickly became the talk of the town, prompting Joe to brave the graffitied streets of the Lower East Side and see what all the fuss was about surrounding his daughter. He couldn't believe his eyes. "I was performing in a leopard G-string and a black tank top," Gaga recounted in *Rolling Stone*. "It wasn't 'She's inappropriate' or 'She's a bad girl' . . . He thought I was nuts, that I was doing drugs and had lost my mind and had no concept of reality anymore. For my father, it was an issue of sanity."

They didn't speak for weeks, as Gaga agonized over the shame of letting him down and the frustration of being misunderstood. Even talking about it five years later, as one of the best-selling pop stars on the planet, brought her to the brink of tears during an interview on MTV. "I remember feeling really sad . . . But then I also remember thinking to myself, 'Someday he will understand why I did all of this.' And I was right."

DATE WITH DESTINY

The devastation of being dropped by Def Jam Records in 2006 felt like the end of her dreams. But when Gaga retreated to her safe haven, the comfort of her grandmother's house in New Jersey, Angelina Germanotta gave her some tough love: "She looked at me, and she goes, 'I'm going to let you cry for the rest of the day, and then you have to stop crying, and you have to go kick some ass.'"

The aspiring singer sat there sobbing, flipping through the channels on TV, until she landed on MTV, which was playing a Destiny's Child music video. "I remember watching Beyoncé thinking, 'Oh, she's a star. I want that. I want to be on MTV,'" Gaga recalled in the special *Inside the Outside*, which aired on the iconic channel in 2011 —two years after she starred in not one but *two* visuals with Queen Bey. By then, MTV had dropped the "music video" from its branding, so the divas' duets—"Video Phone" from *I Am . . . Sasha Fierce* and *The Fame Monster's* "Telephone"—premiered on YouTube, where they have a combined six hundred million views and counting.

THE FAME GAME

If Lady Gaga wasn't going to change for her father, she certainly wasn't going to change for record executives. In the spring of 2007, months after she was dropped by Def Jam, she was summoned to the Los Angeles offices of Interscope to meet with CEO Jimmy Iovine—and showed up wearing a cropped T-shirt, short shorts, and go-go boots. He ended up rescheduling, and two weeks later Gaga returned, this time in a gray tank and red shorts with white suspenders. Iovine was more concerned with how she sounded and apparently liked what he heard, because he signed her on the spot.

MEDIA OUTLETS WENT AHEAD AND CROWNED HER "'THE NEXT QUEEN OF POP.'"

Interscope recognized that Gaga was blessed with not only powerful pipes but also a knack for crafting pop songs (Iovine even compared her to Carole King). As she worked on her own music with Moroccan-Swedish producer RedOne, the singer also wrote material for established chart-toppers Britney Spears, the Pussycat Dolls, and Fergie. One project paired Gaga with multiplatinum artist Akon, who immediately realized her talents were being wasted behind the scenes and negotiated a joint venture with Interscope to sign her to his own KonLive label. "When I see a star, I just know it," Akon told *Entertainment Weekly*. "From the moment she walked in [for our first meeting], her appearance and her attitude felt brand new and fresh. She was so fearless."

When the Senegalese-American singer stopped by the studio and heard three songs Gaga and RedOne had written—"Poker Face," "LoveGame," and "Just Dance"—he stopped in his tracks. "I want to take these songs to Jimmy so we can make her a priority," Akon told RedOne, as he reminisced to *EW*. In Iovine's office, the exec was also thrilled with the songs—but had another act in mind to record "Just Dance": the Pussycat Dolls. "No! It's Gaga," insisted Akon. "She can be the next big thing!" Fortunately, Iovine relented, and the rest is history.

"Just Dance" was released in April 2008 as the lead single off Lady Gaga's forthcoming debut, *The Fame*, an electro-pop dance album with a throwback 1970s sound that ushered in a new era of mainstream radio. On the heels of international smash "Just Dance"—which remains one of the best-selling singles of all time, with over ten million copies sold—"Poker Face," "LoveGame," and "Paparazzi" all went straight to the top of the charts and made *The Fame* a commercial success. Lady Gaga was everywhere: *Saturday Night Live*, the MTV Video Music Awards, the Grammy Awards, *Total Request Live*, *American Idol*, *The Today Show*, *The Tonight Show*. The cover of *Rolling Stone* heralded "The Rise of Lady Gaga," while countless other media outlets went ahead and crowned her "the next Queen of Pop."

She was an unconventional pop star, however: Lady Gaga was provocative, sang about drugs and sex, wore bizarre fashions, and prioritized artistic vision over commercial success. "What has been lost in pop music these days is the combination of the visual and the imagery of the artist, along with the music—and both are just as important," she explained to MTV News in 2008. "So, even though the carefree nature of the album is something that people are latching onto right away about my

stuff, I hope they will take notice of the interactive, multimedia nature of what I'm trying to do. The things I like to do and the theatrics, I like to incorporate them into the choreography. With my music, it's a party, it's a lifestyle, and it's about making the lifestyle the forefront of the music."

In 2009, Gaga revealed the downside of stardom with *The Fame Monster*, an eight-song sequel that sonically surpassed its predecessor: "Bad Romance" sold twelve million copies worldwide and second single "Telephone" was a duet with the one and only Beyoncé. Combined, *The Fame* and *The Fame Monster* sold over eighteen million copies. Gaga celebrated them equally at the Monster Ball, which she described as "the first-ever pop-electro opera." The seven-leg world tour crisscrossed four continents, grossing an estimated $227.4 million. But Gaga was only just beginning. "I feel like I have so much to do," she told *Rolling Stone*. "The whole world sees the number-one records and the rise in sales and recognition, but my true legacy will be the test of time, and whether I can sustain a space in pop culture and really make stuff that will have a genuine impact."

The stakes were high for her second studio album—but no one applied more pressure than Gaga herself. "I want to give my fans nothing less than the greatest album of the decade," she admitted to *Vogue*. "I don't want to give them something trendy. I want to give them the future." She gave millions of Little Monsters a lifeline with 2011's *Born This Way*, specifically its empowering title track, an anthem for the LGBTQ+ community that set an iTunes record with a million copies sold in five days. Other themes found in the lyrics address individualism, sexuality, courage, love, and loss. While helping fans embrace their authentic selves through music, Gaga attempted to do the same for herself. "*Born This Way* is my answer to many questions over the years: Who are you? What are you about?" she revealed to New York's *Metro*. "The most paramount theme on the record is me struggling to understand how I can exist as myself as someone who lives halfway between fantasy and reality all the time."

She artfully explored that inner conflict with the Born This Way Ball, which depicted Lady Gaga as an "alien fugitive" who escaped her home planet for the Kingdom of Fame. At some point during the European leg of the tour, she injured her right hip, but didn't tell anyone. As the tour progressed, each intricately choreographed show exacerbated the labral tear, ultimately creating a hole in her hip the size of a quarter. At a concert in Montreal in February 2013, Gaga struggled to even stand during a "Scheiße" dance sequence. Her body was failing her, and now it was clear to everyone.

Per doctor's orders, the show could no longer go on, and Gaga was forced to cancel the remaining twenty-one dates of the Born This Way Ball. In a message to fans, Mother Monster expressed her devastation for letting them down. "I've been praying it would heal," she confessed. "I hid it from my staff, I didn't want to disappoint my amazing fans. However after last nights [sic] performance I could not walk and still can't."

Gaga underwent immediate surgery and spent the six-month recovery period putting the finishing touches on her next album, *Artpop*, her most experimental work to date. Lead single "Applause" sounds like a narcissist's theme song, but it's actually Gaga's thank-you to the Little Monsters who kept her going through the most excruciating physical pain. "I started breaking and I didn't know what was wrong with me," she revealed on Sirius XM's *The Morning Mash Up*. "But it was the applause that kept me going . . . their passion kept me alive."

"I HATED BEING FAMOUS"

For years, Lady Gaga chased fame, and almost overnight she got exactly what she was looking for. But once the excitement wore off, she craved the life she led before. "I hid a lot . . . to preserve my image as a superstar to my fans," she revealed to the *Guardian* in 2013, five years after "Just Dance" made her a household name. "And it really drove me crazy. So I've really had to make more of an effort to go out more."

But two years later, she still struggled. "I miss going anywhere and meeting a random person and saying hi, and having a conversation about life," she tearfully confessed on *CBS Sunday Morning* in 2015. Gaga then admitted in a 2020 *CBS Sunday Morning* interview that she would go into "just total panic, full-body pain. I'm braced because I'm so afraid. It's like I'm an object, I'm not a person." The stress forced her out of the public eye almost altogether until, ultimately, she found peace in the one thing that had brought all the fame: making music. With 2020's *Chromatica*, "I finally, slowly started to make music and tell my story through my record."

MOTHER OF REINVENTION

For Gaga, *Artpop* was the culmination of her artistry, an aural body of art showcasing her brilliance, innovation, and maturity as a songwriter. She truly believed the album would refine her eccentric image and convince any remaining detractors that she was a true artist. Instead, it only provided them with more fodder. Critics labeled *Artpop* "underwhelming" (*The Independent*), "half-finished" (*Digital Spy*), and "wildly unoriginal" (*The Daily Telegraph*). Even the music bible, *Rolling Stone*, panned it as "a bizarre album of squelchy disco."

Music fans seemed to agree: *Artpop* sold a scant 2.5 million copies, a fraction of *The Fame*'s 14 million—and far less than half of her previous album, *Born This Way*. It seemed Lady Gaga's popularity had, well, popped. Her idol Andy Warhol famously said everyone could achieve fifteen minutes of fame. Was her time up?

"I became very depressed at the end of 2013," she admitted to *Harper's Bazaar*. "I was exhausted fighting people off. I couldn't even feel my own heartbeat. I was angry, cynical and had this deep sadness like an anchor dragging everywhere I go . . . I really felt like I was dying—my light completely out." The first day of 2014, she looked in the mirror and encouraged herself to keep creating. "I said to myself, 'Whatever is left in there, even just one light molecule, you will find it and make it multiply. You have to, for you. You have to, for your music. You have to, for your fans and your family.' . . . I'm lucky I found one little glimmer stored away."

Gaga channeled her creative and personal frustrations into uncharted territories, tapping into passions that had lain dormant within the pop star. As far back as childhood, she had loved jazz. For years, she fantasized about collaborating with Tony Bennett on an album of classics with "a modern twist." The stars finally aligned in 2014, when the two recorded *Cheek to Cheek*, a collection of timeless standards by George Gershwin, Cole Porter, and Irving Berlin. A match made in musical heaven, the duo's album debuted at No. 1 on the *Billboard* 200 chart. The same critics who dismantled *Artpop* a year earlier were now singing Gaga's praises. But more importantly, she had been artistically reborn.

After nearly a decade of producers and record executives telling her to diminish her vocal talents in order to be more radio-friendly, she felt liberated by jazz—as she rebelled against pop music. "There's a part of me that has been quiet for a long time that is now being reawakened," Gaga revealed to the *Sydney Morning Herald*. "My vocal presence has been kind of the smallest presence about me for a long time." It was eighty-seven-year-old Bennett who suggested to the twenty-nine-year-old that she hadn't yet reached her full potential with her pop albums. "He said: 'Hey, you're so much better than you're even letting yourself be,'" Gaga recalled. The opportunity to work with Bennett on *Cheek to Cheek* had "let a wild animal out of a cage."

She fully unlocked her vocal capacity at the 2015 Academy Awards, stealing the show with a medley of songs from *The Sound of Music* as a tribute to Julie Andrews for the film's fiftieth anniversary. Ten days before the show, worried that her performance might "offend" Andrews, Gaga made a call to the legend for her blessing. "She said she'd been working so hard and she was singing everything in my keys," Andrews recalled to *People*. "I said, 'Why? They're very high, even for me.' And she said, 'Because I wanted to honor you, so I did them in your keys.' That seemed like going one step beyond any place she needed to go."

Gaga's next project, however, would have nothing to do with music. That fall, she starred in the fifth season of *American Horror Story* as the Countess, a century-old glamorous vampire who sustains herself on the blood of her human sex partners at the Hotel Cortez in Los Angeles. Mother Monster was cast in the ghoulish role after calling series creator Ryan Murphy. "I told him I wanted a place to put all of my anguish and rage and that I was excited to play a killer," she recalled to *Billboard* as the publication's 2015 Woman of the Year. Murphy added, "We relate to each other because we're both transformers. We do something trying to work out shit in our personal life." Gaga certainly exorcised some demons—and she has the Golden Globe Award for Best Actress (Miniseries or Television Film) to prove it.

Lady Gaga had proven herself as a legitimate singer and actress. But she wasn't ready to return to pop music just yet. At the age of thirty, she reached deeper into her bag of tricks for 2016's *Joanne*, her most autobiographical album yet, which toned down her sound and style. Lead single "Perfect Illusion" introduced a restrained version of Lady Gaga that revived her rock roots but without the theatrical costumes, makeup, and wigs. Less was more: *Joanne*, named after her late aunt, "is a progression for me," Gaga told *People*. "It was about going into the studio and forgetting that I was famous." The spirit of Joanne Germanotta, who died at nineteen from lupus, was the guiding force of the album, as her niece surrendered to the impact of the family's loss and ultimately found closure for her own personal pain.

"Making an album where I was able to just focus on being my father's daughter, being a member of my family, being my friends's friend . . . I was able to put myself back in a place where I am just a human being," Gaga revealed in an interview on Sirius XM. "I realized that all that emotional pain in my voice, all that trauma from my life, all the loss . . . those are the things that connect me to people. It's actually not these images or social media or my fame at all. The thing that really makes me connected to my fans and the world is what I've been through as a human and I had to put that in this record."

BEHIND THE SCENES

Lady Gaga peeled back the curtain with *Five Foot Two*, a 2017 documentary that gave fans an exclusive peek at one of the most challenging years of her life, during the making of *Joanne*. In the opening scene, she got candid about her rocky romance with fiancé Taylor Kinney, whom she met on the set of the music video for "Yoü and I" in 2011. When they eventually split, the doc also captured audio of her raw emotions: "I just want to make music and make people happy, and, like, I'm on tour and I have a family and I just can never get it all right at the same time . . . My love life's imploded."

The singer also revealed the chronic physical pain stemming from her 2013 hip surgery. The day of Tony Bennett's ninetieth birthday celebration, she wept in agony on a couch as she described the excruciating spasms gripping the entire right side of her body. Later, Gaga fought through the pain to headline the 2017 Super Bowl Halftime Show. "It doesn't get bigger than this," says Gaga in the finale of *Five Foot Two*. "What do I do after this?"

FREE WOMAN

For years, Lady Gaga and Bradley Cooper mingled at many of the same Hollywood events, yet they never met. In April 2016, the actor had just signed on to direct the remake of *A Star Is Born* when his leading lady suddenly materialized right in front of him, on a revolving stage belting out "New York, New York." Gaga was the entertainment at the launch of the Parker Institute for Cancer Immunotherapy, performing a medley of her hits and jazz standards for the A-list crowd. Cooper had never seen her sing live before and was floored by her talent.

Gaga's rendition of "La Vie en Rose" by Édith Piaf that night "demolished the room," Cooper recalled to *Billboard*. "I knew that was plutonium." The moment was so powerful, he recreated it in the film, when his character, Jackson, a hard-drinking rock star, first sees Gaga's Ally—singing in a drag bar, in true Mother Monster fashion.

Before Gaga, several other pop stars were in the running to be the star in question, following in the footsteps of icons Judy Garland and Barbra Streisand, who both portrayed incarnations of the character in previous films. Over the two decades *A Star Is Born* was in development at Warner Bros., Whitney Houston, Beyoncé, and Adele had all been in contention. But when fate put Cooper in the audience of a Lady Gaga concert, he knew he had found his Ally. The next day, they officially met (at her home in Malibu, where she made him spaghetti and meatballs) and the more Cooper learned about Lady Gaga, the more Ally became an extension of the superstar.

A decade earlier, as she worked to land a record deal, Gaga had been repeatedly told she was not "pretty enough" to be a famous singer—a subjective snub that fueled her obsession with fame on her debut album. Life imitated art in *A Star Is Born*: Ally gives up on her music dreams because she too has heard that she doesn't have the looks to be a star, especially because her nose is too big. Gaga defined her character with other nods to her own rising star, like her natural mousy brown hair (which she dyed blonde because a record executive worried she looked too much like Amy Winehouse). She also guided Cooper through an improvisational rock star boot camp, not only to be Jackson onscreen but in the recording studio as well. During filming, Gaga and Cooper wrote original songs for the soundtrack inspired by Jackson and Ally's struggles, including "Shallow," which spent forty-five weeks on the *Billboard* Hot 100 chart and won two Grammys in 2019. The singer received an Academy Award nomination for Best Actress and she made history with the film's soundtrack, becoming the first woman to win an Oscar, Grammy, BAFTA, and Golden Globe in a single year.

Gaga carried Ally with her onto her next album, 2020's *Chromatica*, a return to the electro-pop dance music that had made Lady Gaga famous back in 2008. But for the superstar, its lyrical content held much deeper meaning. With this album, she focused on her mental health journey, beginning with an incident that occurred early in her career. At the age of nineteen, she was sexually assaulted by a music producer, a trauma that inspired "Free Woman," about reclaiming her identity as a survivor. Gaga felt so connected to the song, she tentatively named her album *Free Woman*, but it ultimately felt insincere, as she still struggled with PTSD from the assault. The first single, "Rain on Me," a duet with Ariana Grande, was a metaphor for the tears she'd shed, as well as her dependency on alcohol to numb her pain.

Gaga's bravery resonated with Little Monsters, as *Chromatica* debuted at No. 1 on the *Billboard* 200 chart. Commercially, the album didn't come close to achieving the impossibly high bar set by *The Fame*, but critically, it earned its own distinction. Released two months into the coronavirus pandemic, "it's safe to say that *Chromatica* will be the soundtrack for countless quarantine parties," declared *Variety*.

Hollywood called again in 2021, when Gaga starred in *House of Gucci*, a biographical crime drama about the murderous plot to control the Italian fashion label. She spent six months working on an Italian accent and developing her character, Patrizia Reggiani, who was convicted of hiring a hit man to kill her husband in 1995.

Before returning to music, Gaga indulged her dark side in 2024, starring as Harley Quinn in *Joker: Folie à Deux*, the musical sequel to Joaquin Phoenix's 2019 blockbuster, tracing the Batman villain's origins. The singer was so inspired by her character that she recorded an entire musical companion piece to the film, *Harlequin*—as well as the long-awaited *LG7*. For her thirty-eighth birthday on March 28, she gave fans the gift of a promising update. "I am writing some of my best music in as long as I can remember," the singer captioned a smiling selfie. "I can't believe I still get to do what I love. This year will be an important and meaningful year for us I know."

In May, her Chromatica Ball concert film on HBO ended with an eight-second clip of a mysterious new song over a screen reading "LG7 Gaga Returns." Two months later, she celebrated her performance at the Paris Olympics opening ceremony with a second sneak peek. As fans gathered outside her hotel, Gaga emerged from the open roof of a stretch limousine with her laptop to play snippets of not one but two tracks, both of which could barely be heard over the roar of the crowd. As fans awaited LG7, Gaga dropped "Die with a Smile," a soft rock duet with Bruno Mars, that August.

Finally, in the September issue of *Vogue*, Gaga confirmed that *LG7*, "a new pop record," would be released in February 2025. "For a long time, for most of my career, my life was controlled by this business: what people wanted from me; what they hoped I could achieve; how to keep me going," Gaga told the magazine. "And that can be a lot of pressure and it's scary. But I feel like I'm finally coming out on the other side."

BEAUTY OF BUSINESS

Lady Gaga entered the beauty arena in 2019 with Haus Laboratories, her vegan and cruelty-free cosmetics brand. The debut collection featured six kits of lip and eye makeup with names like Haus of Chained Ballerina, Haus of Bitch, and Haus of Metal Head, and later expanded to include a *Chromatica*-themed Stupid Love Palette, glittery lip liners, and bronzer-highlighter duos.

In its first year, Haus Laboratories earned $141.7 million, making it the celebrity makeup brand with the third-highest media value of 2020, behind Rihanna's Fenty Beauty and Kylie Jenner's Kylie Cosmetics. To keep up, the company rebranded as Haus Labs by Lady Gaga in 2022 and launched an elevated line of products, including Triclone Skin Tech Foundation in fifty shades, PHD Hybrid Lip Oil, and Hy-Power Pigment Paints packed with moisturizing, plant-derived squalane and hyaluronic acid.

While dealing with chronic pain from fibromyalgia, Gaga discovered topical arnica cream—and Haus Labs developed a patent-pending fermented arnica to relieve inflammation. "People told me I couldn't do it and I love when people tell me that I can't do things," she said, "because it just makes me want to prove them wrong."

PART TWO

Face the Music

DISCOGRAPHY

As one of the world's best-selling artists, Lady Gaga has music for every mood. Her electro-pop debut, *The Fame*, and its darker sister album, *The Fame Monster*, were made for dance parties. *Born This Way* is an audible boost of empowerment. Little Monsters can explore the avant-garde with *Artpop*, introspection is the core of the emotional *Joanne*, and *Chromatica* is a musical pursuit of healing. "I will do whatever it takes to make the world dance and smile," Gaga told *Paper* magazine. "So if you're in pain and listening to this music, just know that I know what it's like to be in pain. And I know what it's like to also not let it ruin your life."

THE FAME

LADY GAGA STEPS INTO THE SPOTLIGHT

RELEASE DATE: APRIL 19, 2008

• TRACK LIST •

1. Just Dance
(featuring Colby O'Donis)

2. LoveGame

3. Paparazzi

4. Poker Face

5. Eh, Eh
(Nothing Else I Can Say)

6. Beautiful, Dirty, Rich

7. The Fame

8. Money Honey

9. Starstruck

10. Boys Boys Boys

11. Paper Gangsta

12. Brown Eyes

13. I Like It Rough

14. Summerboy

15. Disco Heaven

OLD SCHOOL: A self-described "retrosexual," Lady Gaga was heavily influenced by the sounds of the 1970s and '80s on *The Fame*: synthesizers, electronic beats, glam rock, Studio 54, and artists like David Bowie, Blondie, Queen, Grace Jones, and Madonna. As for the album's title and theme, "I was just reading tabloids like they were textbooks," she told CNN in 2009. "I would buy every scandal book, every paper, every magazine that I could get my hands on, and I would tear sheets out of imagery . . . I embrace pop culture, the very thing that everybody says is poisonous and ostentatious and shallow. It's like my chemistry book."

HAPPY DANCE: Gaga was hungover yet inspired when she sat down to write party ode "Just Dance," knocking it out in just ten minutes. At the time, the twenty-two-year-old was newly signed to Interscope after being dropped by Def Jam and desperate to make noise at her new label. She left New York for Hollywood to work with a new production team, made up of rapper Akon and RedOne, a Moroccan-Swedish producer who was relatively unknown in the United States. "I was in such a dark space in New York. I was so depressed, always in a bar," Gaga revealed to the *Guardian*. "I got on a plane to LA to do my music and was given one shot to write the song that would change my life and I did."

She crafted "Just Dance," a catchy "happy record" that hit the Top 10 in two dozen countries and became one of the best-selling singles of all time, with over ten million copies sold. "Everyone is looking for a song that really speaks to the joy in our souls and in our hearts and having a good time," Gaga reasoned to *ArtistDirect*. "It's just one of those records. It feels really good, and when you listen to it, it makes you feel good inside. It's as simple as that. I don't think it's rocket science when it comes to the heart."

QUEEN OF HEARTS: Gaga combined sex and gambling for "Poker Face," a jackpot of innuendos hinting at her own bisexuality. Backing vocals are provided by RedOne, who sings a line written by Gaga celebrating a female love interest, meant to add "an undertone of confusion"—just like Gaga's poker face. In the bridge, an iconic lyric about Gaga's "muffin" is about faking it "when I was making love to my old boyfriend," she explained on *Friday Night with Jonathan Ross*. "I used to think about women sometimes. I actually never told him but I'm sure he's watching now." He was, and in 2021 the singer provided an update at her Las Vegas residency, *Jazz & Piano*: "He called me and he said, 'Do you know I had to explain this to my mother?'"

JOY RIDE: Disco balls are one thing . . . but what's a disco stick? Gaga explained to *Rolling Stone* that she coined the now infamous "LoveGame" euphemism for male genitalia after developing a "sexual crush" on a stranger at a nightclub. "I said to them, 'I wanna ride on your disco stick.' The next day, I was in the studio, and I wrote the song in about four minutes. When I play the song live, I have an actual stick—it looks like a giant rock-candy pleasuring tool—that lights up." The famed prop also had a starring role in the "LoveGame" music video and has appeared in Gaga's various tours over the years.

VILLAGE VOICE: Although she was well on her way to fame and fortune, Gaga recalled her years of struggling—and partying too much on the Lower East Side—in "Beautiful, Dirty, Rich." "On the Lower East Side, there was a lot of rich kids who did drugs and said that they were poor artists, so it's also a knock at that," she revealed to DJ Ron Slomowicz. "I used to hear my friends on the phone with their parents, asking for money before they would go buy drugs." Still, the song had mass appeal. She added, "No matter who you are and where you come from, you can feel beautiful and dirty rich."

ROCKY ROMANCE: Fame is the theme of Gaga's debut, most obviously on fourth single "Paparazzi," a love song about her equal desire for love and the flash of the cameras. In the lyrics, she's her boyfriend's biggest fan, the groupie to his rock star, in a relationship defined by velvet ropes, guitars, and cigarettes. Art imitated life: Gaga was infatuated with heavy-metal drummer Lüc Carl, whom she dated on and off from 2005 to 2011. He was her first real love, and their initial split in 2009 was devastating for the singer. "I was his Sandy and he was my Danny, and I just broke," she revealed to *Rolling Stone*.

Gaga channeled the pain into the music video for "Paparazzi," casting Alexander Skarsgård as her love interest, who attempts to kill her in front of the cameras and ruins her music career. In the end, she gets revenge by poisoning him—and regains fame as a murderer.

BLOCKBUSTER DEBUT: *The Fame* starred at No. 1 on *Billboard*'s Dance/ Electronic Albums chart for a record-breaking 180 nonconsecutive weeks and was nominated for Album of the Year at the 2010 Grammys (though it lost to Taylor Swift's *Fearless*). Nearly two decades later, Gaga's first showing remains among the most popular: *The Fame* made *Rolling Stone*'s list of the 100 Greatest Debut Albums of All Time, and in 2023, *Billboard* named it the twelfth-biggest album ever on its charts.

THE FAME MONSTER

THE DOWNSIDE TO FAME AND FORTUNE
RELEASE DATE: NOVEMBER 18, 2009

• TRACK LIST •

1. Bad Romance

2. Alejandro

3. Monster

4. Speechless

5. Dance in the Dark

6. Telephone
(featuring Beyoncé)

7. So Happy I Could Die

8. Teeth

MOTHER MONSTER: Lady Gaga's fascination with horror and 1950s sci-fi films inspired this EP's darker concept. "I have an obsession with death and sex. Those two things are also the nexus of horror films," she explained to the *Daily Star*. "I've just been noticing a resurgence of this idea of monster, of fantasy, but in a very real way."

HITCHCOCK BLONDE: The cinephile has talked about her love of the Master of Suspense, Alfred Hitchcock. "I imagine I would have been one of Hitchcock's groupies," Gaga told Jimmy Fallon in 2015. But back in 2009, she wrote him a love letter of sorts in lead single "Bad Romance," name-dropping three of his films—*Psycho*, *Vertigo*, and *Rear Window*—in one lyric.

As the title suggests, "Bad Romance" is about Gaga's attraction to unhealthy relationships, a theme found in many Hitchcock films, which also often juxtapose sex and violence. *Psycho* (1960) is famous for its shower scene, as a nude Marion Crane (Janet Leigh) is stabbed to death by Norman Bates (Anthony Perkins). In *Vertigo* (1958)—a film Gaga has referenced in two music videos—Scottie's (James Stewart) psychological obsession with Judy (Kim Novak) causes her death. Stewart, a frequent Hitchcock collaborator, also starred in 1954's *Rear Window*, playing a man who witnesses a neighbor murdering his bedridden wife.

FASHION, BABY: The music video for "Bad Romance" introduced Gaga the Fashion Muse, with several exclusive pieces from Alexander McQueen's Plato's Atlantis collection. They were the designer's thank-you to Gaga for premiering her song at his Paris Fashion Week show. The closing look, an iridescent dress with a balloon skirt, hits the "Bad Romance" video's catwalk during the bridge, as she steps out in McQueen's twelve-inch (30 cm) Armadillo stilettos. "When I saw this in person, I nearly fell over," Gaga revealed in a 2015 commentary on her YouTube channel. "I said, 'What was he thinking sending this to me?'" McQueen also provided a bronze embossed mini dress, a black dress with leather panels, twelve-inch (30 cm) Dragon heels, and alien-inspired sculpted pumps in white and black—all of which Gaga wore in "Bad Romance" directed by Francis Lawrence.

BAD CONNECTION: After appearing on the remix of Beyoncé's "Video Phone," Gaga recruited Queen B for a duet of "Telephone"—arguably one of the most iconic collaborations in pop music history. But it almost didn't happen. Gaga originally wrote the track for Britney Spears, who passed on recording it for 2008's *Circus* (which does include the Gaga-penned "Quicksand"). "Telephone" was one of the best-selling songs of 2010 and earned a Grammy nomination for Best Pop Collaboration with Vocals, yet Gaga wasn't happy with how it turned out. "I hate 'Telephone,'" she admitted to *Pop Justice*. "Is that terrible to say? It's the song I have the most difficult time listening to . . . But ultimately the mix and the process of getting the production finished was very stressful for me. So when I say it's my worst song it has nothing to do with the song, just my emotional connection to it."

MYSTERY MEN: The "monster" that inspired "Alejandro" is not one particular person but Gaga's general "fear of men," she confessed to *Fuse*. In the lyrics, she does name three of them: Alejandro, Fernando, and Roberto—aka fashion designer Alexander McQueen, producer Fernando Garibay, and producer Rob Fusari, respectively. McQueen and Garibay were close friends and collaborators of Gaga's, and she did have a romantic connection to Fusari, who wrote and produced five tracks on *The Fame*. A year after "Alejandro," Fusari revealed an ugly side when he sued Gaga for $30 million, on the grounds he had "radically" shaped the Grammy winner's career as her business partner, yet she refused to pay him royalties. Gaga countersued, and months later the two settled out of court.

In the "Alejandro" video, which she described to *The Times* as "a celebration and an admiration of gay love," Gaga wears a custom opera coat, dress, and boots designed by McQueen as an ode to her dear friend, who had taken his life just a few months earlier. "I am here today not just because of my talent, but because he believed in me," she said of McQueen. "My weird brand of art pop manic expression of my emotions was the part of me he knew he taught me. I will be grateful long after I pass and join him wherever it is they put souls like us."

DOUBLE TAKE: How did fame change Lady Gaga? She illustrated the "before" and "after" with the two covers of *The Fame Monster*, shot by fashion photographer (and Yves Saint Laurent creative director) Hedi Slimane. The pre-*Fame* version is Stefani Germanotta, a brunette with black tears streaming from one eye. *Fame Monster*'s cover shows off a blonde in an exaggerated wig and black vinyl coat pulled up to partially obscure her face. When her record label saw the photos, executives argued the "before" gothic Gaga was "too dark" and "not pop," she recalled to *Rolling Stone*. "I said, 'You don't know what pop is, because everyone was telling me I wasn't pop last year, and now look—so don't tell me what pop is, I know what pop is.'"

MONSTER MEMORABILIA: In addition to *The Fame Monster* EP, the eight songs were packaged with *The Fame* as a deluxe double album that came with plenty of Gaga goodies, including the *Book of Gaga*, a puzzle, paper dolls, 3D glasses, behind-the-scenes photos . . . and a lock of hair from one of her wigs. "I get to wear my real hair now because it is super-healthy, but I have worn a lot of wigs and I just said to the guys, 'Why don't you just give away locks of my hair?'" Gaga joked, according to *Digital Spy*. "Some people are saying it is creepy, but they don't know my fans."

GAGA AT THE GARDEN

Lady Gaga's two-night engagement at New York's Madison Square Garden in February 2011 was so epic, cameras captured it all for an HBO special that won a Primetime Emmy Award. *Lady Gaga Presents the Monster Ball Tour: At Madison Square Garden* is a high-definition look at the singer onstage and off, weaving Technicolor concert footage with behind-the-scenes moments (shot in black and white) that spotlight the Manhattan native's full-circle success. The two-hour television special pulled in 1.2 million viewers and plenty of critical acclaim, most surprisingly from the conservative *New York Post*. "Forget the usual pyrotechnics of today's pop concerts," declared reviewer Linda Stasi. "By the end of this show, Gaga has fire shooting out of her boobs and her crotch—and, somehow, by then it's not even surprising. It's just terrific." *Lady Gaga Presents the Monster Ball Tour: At Madison Square Garden* was also released on DVD, Blu-Ray, and digitally on iTunes, with even more previously unseen footage, and spent 64 weeks on *Billboard*'s Top Music Video chart.

BORN THIS WAY

A CALL FOR ACCEPTANCE
RELEASE DATE: MAY 21, 2011

• TRACK LIST •

1. Marry the Night
2. Born This Way
3. Government Hooker
4. Judas
5. Americano
6. Hair
7. Scheiße
8. Bloody Mary
9. Bad Kids
10. Highway Unicorn (Road to Love)
11. Heavy Metal Lover
12. Electric Chapel
13. Yoü and I
14. The Edge of Glory

HIGH NOTE: Lady Gaga's second studio album is an ambitious opus and anthem of equality that remains a high note of her discography. To match the heavier lyrical content surrounding sex and gender, she broadened the scope of her dance-pop repertoire with flashes of heavy metal ("Electric Chapel"), rock and roll ("Yoü and I"), and opera ("Government Hooker"). "It's quite eclectic. It ranges from 'Born This Way' being very light to the rest of the album becoming quite darker," Gaga explained to *Billboard*. "I in jest say that 'Born This Way' is the marijuana to the heroins of the album, the ultimate intense intoxication of the record."

MOTORCYCLE MAMA: The shape-shifting artist illustrated "I'm endlessly always changing" on the cover of *Born This Way*, which depicts Gaga as half-human half-motorcycle, with her head as the headlight. Fans weren't exactly riding with the image, described by the *Guardian* as "more like a cheap Photoshop job than the most anticipated album of the year." Little Monsters flooded message boards and social media to express confusion. Did this mean Gaga had been born a motorcycle? Despite the widespread scorn, she recreated the cover art night after night on the Born This Way Ball during "Heavy Metal Lover."

MOTHER OF REINVENTION: Gaga's freedom song for all Little Monsters, "Born This Way," espouses self-acceptance and pride. Mother Monster brought that message to life in the music video, a "surrealist painting" inspired by Salvador Dalí and Francis Bacon that gave new meaning to "born this way" with the opening image, in which Gaga gives birth to a new race, her fans. By the end, it's a population of Little Monsters. Fans couldn't wait to get their paws on the video, which was filmed at a top-secret location—and edited inside a hotel suite to prevent any potential leaks. "We couldn't go anywhere," director Nick Knight recalled to *Paper* for *Born This Way*'s tenth anniversary. "Her fans—bless them—are so obsessive about her. We didn't want to risk anything being released beforehand."

SAX GOD: As Gaga put the finishing touches on "Hair," about expressing one's individuality through personal style, the song gave her "a Bruce Springsteen vibe." So she picked up the phone one afternoon and called the man who helped define The Boss's signature E Street sound, his longtime saxophonist Clarence Clemons. "I was so excited," he recalled to *Rolling Stone*, and offered to come by the studio any time. Gaga needed him "right now in New York City"—yet Clemons lived in Florida. The self-described "Gaga-ite" dropped everything and drove to the airport so fast "I almost got a ticket."

When Clemons arrived at the studio at midnight with saxophone in hand, Gaga had just one request: "Play from your heart." He invigorated "Hair" as well as "Edge of Glory" with rousing solos after only a few takes. "I would have done it for free," gushed Clemons. "She's the real deal. All the craziness and stuff, there's a purpose to all of it. She has no boundaries . . . It's a day I'll never forget." The legendary musician even joined Gaga in the music video for "Edge of Glory," which turned out to be his final public appearance. Two days after its release, Clemons died after suffering a massive stroke at his home.

CIRCLE OF LIFE: Gaga returned to New York during a break on the Monster Ball Tour in September 2010 to be with her dying grandfather. The night before he passed away, Gaga and her father Joe sat down at the piano with a bottle of tequila—and by the time it was half empty, she had written "Edge of Glory." As she tinkered with the keys beside him, she offered her father words of comfort: His parents had been married for sixty years and had created a beautiful family—her grandfather had "won at life." "Don't be sad, he's on the edge of the most glorious moment in life," Gaga recalled saying on *Oprah's Next Chapter*. "By the time we got through it, my dad was crying, I was crying."

GAGA'S BABY: The fifth and final single off *Born This Way*, "Marry the Night," was the only one not to reach the Top 10 on the *Billboard* Hot 100 chart. But it's one of Gaga's favorite tracks on the album, inspired by two artists who had the greatest impact on her artistry. "Imagine if Bruce Springsteen had a baby with Whitney Houston—that's what it is," she joked in her MTV documentary *Inside the Outside*. Producer Fernando Garibay conceived the church bell–inspired instrumental after seeing the Monster Ball Tour. "Your show is a religion and your fans are a cult," Garibay told Gaga. "It's this epic music. It's just so big."

ARTPOP

AN AMBITIOUS EFFORT AHEAD OF ITS TIME
RELEASE DATE: NOVEMBER 6, 2013

• TRACK LIST •

1. Aura
2. Venus
3. G.U.Y.
4. Sexxx Dreams
5. Jewels n' Drugs
   (featuring T.I., Too Short, and Twista)
6. MANiCURE
7. Do What U Want
   (featuring R. Kelly)

8. ARTPOP
9. Swine
10. Donatella
11. Fashion!
12. Mary Jane Holland
13. Dope
14. Gypsy
15. Applause

BIG PICTURE: A fan of pop art and pop music, Gaga found a way to merge the two on her experimental third studio album. When she envisioned the title and theme, she also saw the bigger picture. "When I'm thinking about the title for an album, I think about the marketing, I think about the cultural implication of the words, what the words mean," she explained to *Entertainment Weekly*. "How the words will change the meaning after the music has been put out as well as the visuals. I spent some time and I kept seeing those two words, 'art' and 'pop,' put together in a reverse way, instead of pop art, which is the way I had always seen it. And then quite quickly, the more work that I did, *Artpop* became something that had a nice ring, you know?"

BLANK CANVAS: Recorded in 2012, *Artpop* was set for an early 2013 release, but it was delayed when Gaga underwent hip surgery that required six months of rest and rehabilitation. As her body healed, she enriched her mind with books, music, and "creative gifts" she exchanged with her Haus of Gaga collective of fashion, hair, and makeup experts. She also used the forced downtime to fine-tune her album. "I got to put a giant white or black sheet of paint over my whole canvas and I got to review *Artpop* again," she told *Women's Wear Daily*. "I was given the time to really be creative because it's a gazing process, it really is. I have to gaze into the work for long periods of time for it to be good."

ART APPRECIATION: The "Applause" music video is an ode to all the things Gaga applauds: Andy Warhol, the Italian Renaissance, Impressionism, German Expressionist cinema, and her "passion for shapeshifting [sic]" (as she explained on X). Tracing the steps of her career thus far, she brings to life some of the most influential art pieces, from Warhol's "Marilyn Diptych" pop art portrait and Botticelli's *The Birth of Venus* (complete with seashell bra) to pioneering silent sci-fi film *Metropolis* (1927). To illustrate the song's theme, she created her own art: a "glove-kini" bra resembling two hands, custom-made by Jean-Charles de Castelbajac, a collaborator of pop artist Keith Haring.

G.U.Y.S. & WIVES: The music video for "G.U.Y." expanded into an epic twelve-minute short film incorporating "Artpop," "Venus," and

"MANiCURE"—and a cameo from the cast of *The Real Housewives of Beverly Hills*. Shot at Hearst Castle in San Simeon, California, the opulent visual opens with Gaga as a fallen angel shot out of the sky by an arrow. She's brought into the historic castle and baptized in its Neptune Pool while the reality stars serenade her with "Venus." Reborn as a Greek goddess, Gaga proclaims, "Greetings, Himeros, god of sexual desire" and transitions into "G.U.Y." The "Girl Under You" gets amorous by the castle's tiled indoor Roman Pool and resurrects Michael Jackson, Gandhi, John Lennon, and Jesus, only to clone their DNA to create a G.U.Y. army that invades a corporate office with Mother Monster and *Beverly Hills* accomplices Lisa Vanderpump and Kyle Richards. Mission complete, the end credits roll to the tune of "MANiCURE."

SECOND THOUGHTS: Second single "Do What U Want" is a collaboration with R. Kelly, an R&B-electropop bop written in response to gossip about Gaga's fluctuating weight. The chart-topper was polarizing, considering the repeated accusations of sexual abuse against the "I Believe I Can Fly" singer. But when TMZ reported raunchy details from the set of the music video (directed by Terry Richardson, who has faced sexual misconduct allegations of his own), unease with Kelly's involvement reached a fever pitch—and Gaga not only scrapped the visual but also recorded an alternate version of "Do What U Want" with Christina Aguilera to replace the original on future vinyl and CD pressings. Five years later, when the Lifetime series *Surviving R. Kelly* documented even more disturbing allegations, Gaga pulled the song from all streaming platforms.

CULT CLASSIC: Compared to other 2013 releases like *Beyoncé* and Katy Perry's *Prism*, *Artpop* was considered a commercial failure with 2.5 million albums sold in the first year, a discourse Gaga rejected. "I'm sorry I didn't sell a million records the first week," she said at SXSW. "I have before. I've sold 27 million albums. I'm very proud of what we did. I've sold as much as everybody else sells. I'm held to such an insane standard; it's almost like everybody forgets where the music business is now."

ARTPOP 2: Gaga teased an "Act 2" that would split the music into two collections, "Art" (experimental material) and "Pop" (radio-friendly songs). For months, the singer openly mused about whether to release a double album or separate volumes, and if she might incorporate the concept into her Artpop Ball world tour. At the 2014 SXSW festival, Gaga seemingly hinted at a third act—then debated even putting out her unreleased material at all. "There's many volumes of work over a long period of time that have just not been released to the public because I've chosen to not put it into the system," she revealed. "Sometimes it's just fun to have records that me and my friends listen to. We love it. We don't care what everybody else thinks. Maybe one day I'll release them."

Artpop 2 never materialized, but fans haven't forgotten about it. In 2018, ears perked up when Gaga's producer DJ White Shadow made a reference to *Artpop*'s forthcoming "little sister"—which turned out to be 2020's *Chromatica*. Little Monsters took matters into their own paws with a 2021 petition to release the sequel. The undying interest in *Artpop 2* "has inspired such a tremendous warmth in my heart," Mother Monster tweeted, and DJ White Shadow promised fans they would "discuss your wishes." But two years later, he popped everyone's bubble: "I am officially finished," he announced in an Instagram Story. "Don't ask me about it. Don't talk to me about it."

A NEW DIMENSION

At the start of the space tourism trend in 2013, when celebrities like Ashton Kutcher paid top dollar for a ticket aboard Virgin Galactic, Lady Gaga was tapped by Sir Richard Branson to make history as the first artist to perform outside the atmosphere. It was all part of the 2015 Zero G Colony music festival, a three-day celebration of cutting-edge technology at Spaceport America in New Mexico—with Gaga billed as the headlining act. At dawn on the final day, she would blast off aboard a Virgin Galactic SpaceShip Two and perform one song once the spacecraft reached zero gravity. According to *Us Weekly*, Gaga had "taken out a ridiculous life insurance policy" ahead of the risky stunt. She confirmed the rumors at ArtRave, a two-day event in promotion of *Artpop*, telling *Extra* she had no fear because "I'm already on this rollercoaster . . . Space is just the next step into the beyond." Ultimately, she remained on Earth: In 2014, Gaga's performance was canceled when a SpaceShip Two exploded during a test flight, killing the pilot.

JOANNE

GAGA STRIPS AWAY THE THEATRICS
RELEASE DATE: OCTOBER 21, 2016

• TRACK LIST •

1. Diamond Heart

2. A-YO

3. Joanne

4. John Wayne

5. Dancin' in Circles

6. Perfect Illusion

7. Million Reasons

8. Sinner's Prayer

9. Come to Mama

10. Hey Girl
(featuring Florence Welch)

11. Angel Down

DELUXE EDITION

12. Grigio Girls

13. Just Another Day

14. Angel Down (work tape)

MISS AMERICANA: It's Lady Gaga as we'd never heard her before: a stripped-down sound blending soft rock, folk, pop, country, and Americana. As she went in a whole new direction, she brought along a whole new musical team: *Joanne* features the talents of producer Mark Ronson, songwriter Beck ("Dancin' in Circles"), Queens of the Stone Age guitarist Josh Homme, musician Father John Misty, and Florence Welch for a duet on "Hey Girl."

Joanne was two years in the making. In a December 2014 interview with Yahoo!, the singer teased she was working on new, very different music. "I want the fans to be surprised, but I will just tell you that it's a wonderful, soul-searching experience. And it's very unlike the last album in that way. I made that album on the road. *Artpop* was, you know, the acid-making record. And this record is like—my old self as a cadaver. And I'm just, I'm operating on my old self."

FAMILY TIES: Named after her paternal aunt Joanne who died at nineteen from lupus, the autobiographical album is themed around family, the people who shaped Stefani long before she became Lady Gaga. The most influential is the one she never got to meet, whom she eulogizes on the title track "Joanne," a song about healing she describes as "the true heart and soul of the record." Written after she returned home from the grueling Artpop Ball, "It's everything about Joanne . . . it's all the toughness of the pain of losing her that made us all strong and made us who we are," Gaga explained to *People*. "She is the woman of my past who is becoming and helping me bring more of my honest woman self into the future."

Joanne also helped heal old wounds caused by her brother Joe, who for many years did not approve of his daughter's downtown lifestyle and risqué performances. "That's at the center of it, as well: I always wanted to be a good girl," Gaga explained to the magazine. "And Joanne was such a good girl. But I have such a rebellious spirit, and my father was always very angry. He drank because of his sister's death. I was trying to understand him through making this record."

RIDE A COWBOY: Gaga ended her engagement to longtime love Taylor Kinney during the making of *Joanne*, and the anguish is evident on several tracks, most obviously on "Million Reasons," an ode to heartbreak and hope. The newly single singer dives into her relationship patterns on "John Wayne," which features Homme on guitar and dissects "my incessant need to run after wild men and somehow I get bored of the same old John," she confessed to Apple Music's Zane Lowe. But she can be just as wild, evidenced by "Sinner's Prayer": "This song is about singing to a man, just telling him, 'Look, I just don't want to break the heart of any other man but you, but I know that I'm a sinner.'"

THINK PINK: The pink wide-brimmed hat Gaga wears on the cover of *Joanne* became a symbol of this musical era, a stark contrast to her previous eccentric headdresses adorned with lobsters, telephones, and Muppets. Designed by Gladys Tamez, the iconic accessory was inspired by another singer, Mick Jagger's ex Marianne Faithfull, and customized for Gaga in her favorite color. She first fell in love with Tamez's bespoke millinery while wearing the "Lady Dandy" style during her *Joanne* writing sessions. When the album came out, she ordered another thirty in an array of pastel colors, but the pink felt velour with white ribbon remains a classic—and inspired Tamez to create a $680 variation she named the "Lady Joanne."

VIDEO ANTHOLOGY: The four separate visuals created for *Joanne* tell a complete story. The first, for lead single "Perfect Illusion," shows the singer—decked out in a ponytail, black T-shirt embroidered with "Lady Gaga," and teeny-tiny denim shorts—getting up close and personal with fans during a high-energy performance in the desert. The closing shot, Gaga lying on the ground all alone, opens the next video, "Million Reasons," as a fleet of black SUVs rush in to pick up the pop star and whisk her off to the next gig, a video shoot where she dons the pink *Joanne* hat and matching two-piece suit. The country-inspired look carries over into "John Wayne," but only for a moment before she strips down to a series of Lady Gaga–coded looks as she gets pretty reckless with a series of bad boys. When she accidentally kills herself, the "Joanne" persona picks up her guitar and walks into the woods for her own video, the fourth and final in the series. The ode to her aunt is an emotional journey in color and black-and-white, as a makeup-less Gaga wanders through a forest before eventually ending up in a New York pool hall with her sister Natali.

GENERATIONAL TALENT: Like her niece, Joanne Germanotta was a creative spirit who loved to paint and write poetry. In her short lifetime, she didn't get the opportunity to be published, so when Gaga debuted with *The Fame* in 2008, three decades after Joanne's death, she included her aunt's poem "For a Moment" in the album booklet, along with her own octave, "A Poem for Joanne." "For all the words you could not say / I promise they'll be mine," wrote Gaga.

GONE COUNTRY: Gaga is credited with starting a trend among pop stars who experimented with country-inspired sounds, including Justin Timberlake's *Man of the Woods*, Miley Cyrus's *Younger Now*, and Kylie Minogue's *Golden*. However, none achieved the same commercial success as *Joanne*, which debuted at No. 1 on the *Billboard* 200 chart and earned two Grammy nominations.

CHROMATICA

DANCE THROUGH THE EMOTIONAL PAIN
RELEASE DATE: MAY 29, 2020

• TRACK LIST •

1. Chromatica I

2. Alice

3. Stupid Love

4. Rain on Me
   (with Ariana Grande)

5. Free Woman

6. Fun Tonight

7. Chromatica II

8. 911

9. Plastic Doll

10. Sour Candy
    (with BLACKPINK)

11. Enigma

12. Replay

13. Chromatica III

14. Sine from Above
    (with Elton John)

15. 1000 Doves

16. Babylon

CLUB MONSTER: After *Joanne*, a jazz album with Tony Bennett, and the *A Star Is Born* soundtrack, the downtown club kid returned to her music roots for *Chromatica*, a medley of electronica ("Alice"), house ("Sour Candy" with K-pop's BLACKPINK), Eurodisco ("Fun Tonight"), and dance-pop ("Stupid Love"). Released during the COVID-19 lockdown, the album was a bright spot for many fans going through a dark time. "I can't wait to dance with people to this music. I can't wait to just go into any space with a whole bunch of people and blast this as loud as possible to show them how much I love them," Gaga told Apple Music's Zane Lowe. "Until then, I hope they listen to this album . . . but also go through their own journey and dance through all their pain."

ANOTHER WORLD: As Gaga worked through physical, mental, and emotional pain, she escaped to Chromatica, a fictional planet of inclusive people where peace is achieved through dance. And it became the concept for her album. According to Gaga, communities in the extraterrestrial society are differentiated by respective colors, and she aligns with the pink "Kindness Punks" in the music video for *Chromatica*'s lead single, "Stupid Love." As their leader, she brokers peace with a dance battle that ultimately unites all colors of Chromatica's rainbow.

POP REIGN: Two of the most powerful voices in music banded together to wash away their respective traumas on the Grammy-winning "Rain on Me." For Gaga, she was working through chronic PTSD from being sexually assaulted at nineteen, which she publicly revealed a decade later at the height of her career. Ariana Grande's wounds were fresher: Two years earlier, suicide bombers had killed twenty-two fans (and injured a thousand more) as they exited her Manchester Arena concert on May 22, 2017. The following year, on the heels of her split from boyfriend Mac Miller, the rapper died of an accidental drug overdose at the age of twenty-six.

In the recording studio, there were no egos, no diva behavior—just two brave women supporting each other's healing journey through tears and laughs. When it was Ariana's turn to hop on the mic, Mother Monster showered her with encouragement. "'Everything that you care about while you sing, I want you to forget it and just sing,'" Gaga recalled saying to Zane Lowe. "'And by the way, while you're doing that, I'm gonna dance in front of you' . . . and [Ariana] started to do things with her voice that were different. It was the joy of two artists going like, 'I see you.'" Ariana agreed, gushing on social media about their special connection: "I met a woman who knew pain the same way I did . . . who cried as much as I did, drank as much wine as I did, ate as much pasta as I did and [whose] heart was bigger than her whole body . . . She then held my hand and invited me into the beautiful world of Chromatica and together, we got to express how beautiful and healing it feels to mothafuckinnnn cry!"

PAIN KILLER: One of *Chromatica*'s most revealing tracks, "911," sounds the alarm on the singer's mental-health struggles, particularly her dependency on antipsychotic medication. The recording process was ultimately therapeutic, even though she had to relive the trauma with every vocal take. "She wore a wig to the studio that day, hoping it would make it a little bit easier to feel like someone else," producer BloodPop told *Rolling Stone*. "We had it almost pitch-black in the studio. I wish everyone could see what I saw because she really fought for each and every one of these songs to put her whole self into it, at any cost."

THEIR SONG: Gaga sings about the healing power of music with someone who knows "sad songs say so much": Elton John. Collaborating with her longtime friend and mentor on "Sine from Above" was especially poignant because "he's always challenged me to keep my head above water and it's something that I always appreciate," Gaga revealed to Lowe. "He knows when I'm down. . . . And I cannot tell you how instrumental in my life he's been, showing me that you can go all the way in life and . . . be authentic and be you and do good things in the world."

COVER STORY: Like the planet it symbolizes, *Chromatica* is not utopian or dystopian, an interplay of light and dark, according to Gaga's creative director Nicola Formichetti. To illustrate that contrast on the album cover, "We needed something that wasn't running from the past—actually, we wanted to embrace the past—to show that Gaga is on her path towards healing," he told *Vogue*. Shot by German fashion photographer Norbert Schoerner, the arresting image shows pink-haired Gaga strapped to a metal grate, a squiggle-shaped "sine" running over her body to represent sound. Her hands are welded claws; her heeled boots are fashioned from a knife on one foot and an animal horn on the other.

"[The cover] is almost a tableau of different parts of her journey throughout her life," explained Formichetti. "How she has always transformed herself into different characters, establishing these Gaga 'codes.' . . . She's bonded to this fashion. But this isn't a bad thing. It's both about where she started and how far she has come."

A NEW DAWN: The dance party continues on *Dawn of Chromatica*, a 2021 remix album that turns up the volume on hyperpop, an electronic microgenre that originated in the UK in the early 2010s. Aside from "Boom Clap" singer-songwriter Charli XCX (on "911"), the track list's featured artists are mostly underground talent from around the world: Venezuelan producer Arca, Japanese-British multi-threat Rina Sawayama, Brazilian drag queen Pabllo Vittar, and English DJ-rapper Shygirl.

HARLEQUIN

A MUSICAL COMPANION TO *JOKER: FOLIE À DEUX*
RELEASE DATE: SEPTEMBER 27, 2024

• TRACK LIST •

1. Good Morning
2. Get Happy (2024)
3. Oh, When the Saints
4. World on a String
5. If My Friends Could See Me Now
6. That's Entertainment
7. Smile
8. The Joker
9. Folie à Deux
10. Gonna Build a Mountain
11. Close to You
12. Happy Mistake
13. That's Life

NO JOKE: In mid-September 2024, Gaga made several cryptic Instagram posts. "Moondust gets everywhere," read one graphic. "Still not October," noted another, accompanied by a short clip of a rock instrumental. What did it all mean, *Entertainment Tonight* asked Gaga during a *Joker* interview on September 23. She smiled coyly, whispering, "It's a secret." The very next day, she revealed it: *Harlequin*, a companion album to *Joker: Folie à Deux*, named after her character, Harleen "Lee" Quinzel's alter ego, Harley Quinn.

The track list explained Gaga's social media teases. "Moondust gets everywhere" turned out to be a lyrical hint at "Close to You" by the

Carpenters, Track 11 on *Harlequin*. As for the "Still not October" musical sneak peek, that was "The Joker" from the 1964 musical *The Roar of the Greasepaint – The Smell of the Crowd*.

VINTAGE POP: During the making of *Folie à Deux*, Gaga felt a deep connection to Lee that stayed with her long after production wrapped. "She just didn't really leave me creatively, and I decided I wanted to make a whole album inspired by her," Gaga told Apple Music's Zane Lowe. "She's a really complex woman." And yet, somehow, she simplified the recording experience for Gaga. *Harlequin* is technically *LG6.5*, not the long-awaited follow-up to 2020's *Chromatica*, affording the singer complete freedom to experiment with what she dubbed "vintage pop," a blend of jazz, doo-wop, soul, gospel, and rock.

MUSIC FOR TWO: Gaga conceived *Harlequin* with her fiancé, Michael Polansky, and he was instrumental in selecting the album's track list, which includes Charlie Chaplin's "Smile" (first recorded by Nat King Cole in 1954), "If My Friends Could See Me Now" from Broadway's *Sweet Charity*, and Christian hymn "Oh, When the Saints." One of the oldest songs is 1930's "Get Happy," popularized by Judy Garland in the 1950 MGM musical *Summer Stock*. To bring it into the twenty-first century for *Folie à Deux*, "We focused on deploying slapstick and lyrical changes in reference to Arthur," Joaquin Phoenix's character who takes on the Joker persona, Gaga told *Entertainment Weekly*. "The lyric, 'If a nice guy can lose, what's it matter if you win?'—that's pretty daring, considering who Arthur is, what he's done, and it's something the film grapples with. We're rooting for Arthur, and yet he killed five people. That lyric change on 'Get Happy' creates a context that I think is super interesting and makes the song more manic and celebratory in the spirit of the contrast and tension of the circumstances in the movie."

LADY & LEE: Of the album's thirteen tracks, two are Lady Gaga originals written in the spirit of Lee and her descent into madness. While crazy-love waltz "Folie à Deux" seamlessly blends into *Harlequin*'s vintage vibe, "Happy Mistake" is a modern ballad and a highlight of *Harlequin*. Lyrically, it's biographically Gaga and "the way I've split off into personalities throughout my career," she revealed to *EW*. "Playing a strung-out girl my whole career was a way for me to split off from my true self, but, it's all me. Basically, that song says if I was ever going to find joy or happiness in my life, it would probably feel like an accident. Where I was in my life for a long time, I was on a path that was pretty futile because I was so split off from reality. My dedicated fans know this about me, that playing a persona had a price, and it has a price for Lee and her love of Joker."

POP ART: The day after announcing the album, Gaga gave fans an eighty-second preview of "The Joker" with a cinematic visual that shows the singer—in her red-hair *Harlequin* era—wandering the Louvre in Paris alone at night. She dances awkwardly among the art until she happens upon the Mona Lisa, to whom she gives a lipstick smile just like she does Arthur in *Folie à Deux*. "The Joker," which has been performed by the likes of Sammy Davis Jr. and Shirley Bassey, is sung from the perspective of a person whom society sees as a joke. But in Gaga's version, Lee gets the last laugh, thanks to her relationship with Arthur/the Joker. "Michael and I wanted to show the defiance of Lee proclaiming that she is the real criminal in all of this," Gaga told *EW*, "and that she has the ability to mastermind a kind of coup d'etat in their relationship, that she is the persona of Joker incarnate, in a woman."

RUNNING GAG: *Harlequin*'s cover art reflects Lee's mental instability: Gaga (in a cropped red wig) stands in a shower fully dressed, with an orange life preserver around her neck. On the back of the album, another photo shows a bedroom littered with garbage, or so it seems. A closer look reveals several Easter eggs hinting at the highs and lows of the singer's own legacy, including the disco-ball bra from the "Just Dance" video, a smashed VHS tape labeled "Joanne World Tour" (which Gaga had to cancel in 2018 due to chronic pain), and a TV broadcasting Tony Bennett, her longtime friend and jazz collaborator who died in 2023.

MONSTER MASH: Following the London premiere of *Folie à Deux*, Gaga hosted a fan-only *Harlequin* listening party at the NoMad. As the clock ticked closer to midnight, Gaga got on the mic to lead the room in a group performance of "Happy Birthday" for her fiancé, Michael, who turned forty-one on September 26. The evening and *Harlequin* were doubly special, she told the crowd, because "this is our first project together."

PART THREE

Gagapedia

GAGA A TO Z

Welcome to the compendium of everything a fan should know about Mother—from pop artist Andy Warhol, her greatest pop culture influence, to Zappa House, the $5.25 million historic Los Angeles estate where she recorded the soundtrack for *A Star Is Born* and *Chromatica*. There's also the story behind her iconic Bubble Dress, her three French bulldogs (Asia, Gustav, and Koji), the Joanne Trattoria family restaurant, her record-breaking Super Bowl Halftime Show, her timeless bond with Tony Bennett, and the yellow wig that defined the Monster Ball Tour. Now you know your ABCs of Gaga . . .

ANDY WARHOL

Where art and celebrity culture intersect is where Andy Warhol flourished as a pop art pioneer. For three decades beginning in the 1960s, the visual artist captured American pop culture in his iconic silkscreen prints, books, movies, and music—and it all had a profound influence on Lady Gaga, who was born the year before Warhol died from cardiac arrhythmia in 1987. As she began to cultivate her image and artistry, "Andy Warhol's books became her bible," friend Darian Darling told *New York Magazine* in 2010. "She would highlight them with a pen."

At the beginning of her music career, she modeled the Haus of Gaga creative team after The Factory, Warhol's hangout for his "superstars," a clique of personalities who popped up in his works. Her debut album, *The Fame*, also takes a cue from Warhol's famous expression that anyone can achieve "fifteen minutes of fame." Gaga of course exceeded that time limit, and for the cover of the album's sequel, *The Fame Monster*, she donned a platinum-blonde wig only slightly more exaggerated than Warhol's infamous hairpiece.

By 2013's *Artpop*, the pop artist had successfully pulled a "reverse" Warhol by putting "art culture into pop music." Gaga was inspired after visiting a Paris art museum and seeing a Warhol painting that didn't look like a Warhol. "I started to cry," she recalled to *Fuse* in 2012, when she realized the artist had been her age when he made it. "And I said, 'I feel like that painting.' I feel like I have not yet defined my aesthetic. So I'm just beginning."

BUBBLE DRESS

It was love at first sight when Hussein Chalayan debuted a minidress made of bubbles in his Spring/Summer 2007 One Hundred and Eleven collection. Two years later, Gaga wanted to include the look in her

"I COULD GO AWAY, AND PEOPLE MIGHT SAY, 'GOSH, WHATEVER HAPPENED TO THAT GIRL WHO NEVER WORE PANTS?'"

The Fame Ball Tour, but "it's, like, half a million dollars in a museum somewhere," she told MTV News. So, she commissioned Muto-Little Costumes to remake it—and also had a clear piano filled with plastic bubbles custom built to match the theme of the show, which the singer hoped would "bring a tremendous feeling and sentiment of escapism."

In an interview with *New York Magazine*, she previewed her first-ever headlining tour, "singing about love and art and the future. I should like to make one person believe in that moment, and it would be worth every salt of a No. 1 record. I can have hit records all day, but who fucking cares? A year from now, I could go away, and people might say, 'Gosh, whatever happened to that girl who never wore pants?' But how wonderfully memorable thirty years from now, when they say, 'Do you remember Gaga and her bubbles?' Because, for a minute, everybody in that room will forget every sad, painful thing in their lives, and they'll just live in my bubble world."

YOU CAN TAKE THE LADY OUT OF THE LOWER EAST SIDE, BUT YOU CAN'T TAKE THE LOWER EAST SIDE OUT OF THE LADY!

Gaga loved the Bubble Dress so much that she wore a few variations of it, including a jacket and bodysuit for the June 11, 2009, cover of *Rolling Stone*. Then, in 2013, there was Bubble Dress 2.0, designed by the TechHaus branch of Haus of Gaga. "Anemone," a 3D-printed creation, integrated several "bubble factories" into the garment, brought to life by fashion and technology company Studio XO. "The dress blows bubbles on its own!" raved Gaga on Twitter (now X). "It feels magical to wear!"

COACHELLA

When Beyoncé revealed she was pregnant with twins and subsequently dropped out of the 2017 Coachella Valley Music and Arts Festival, ticket-holders demanded a worthy replacement for the headlining act. Five days later, Lady Gaga was announced—and she had only two months to put together an epic ninety-minute set. The twenty songs were every Little Monster's dream, with several deep cuts like "Scheiße" and "Teeth" and remixed versions of hit songs "LoveGame," "Just Dance," and "Applause." Beyoncé did make an appearance at Coachella after all: Gaga's duet partner on 2010's "Telephone" seemingly "called in" during her verse, as backup dancers held out telephones while Bey's recorded vocals played over the speakers.

Mother Monster dressed accordingly for the hot desert weather. On Weekend 1, the military-inspired leather Mugler trench coat she wore for opening number "Scheiße" was shed within minutes, revealing a black bodysuit and lace-up boots. Over the ninety minutes, the quick-change artist mixed it up with rainbow sequin boots, a Balenciaga denim jacket, and even her own Coachella merch, a red cropped hoodie. Weekend 2 followed a similar theme: black bodysuit and rainbow sequin shorts, a cropped leather jacket, and a pink cropped hoodie.

Gaga made the most of her time in the Indio, California, desert: In the days between her two headlining weekends, she filmed scenes for *A Star Is Born* in which her character performs at Coachella. Local fans were invited to be extras and instructed to show up decked out in country-themed attire, with just one exception—no pink *Joanne* hats.

DIVE BARS

You can take the lady out of the Lower East Side, but you can't take the Lower East Side out of the lady! During Gaga's early years of trying to make a name for herself in the downtown New York scene, she was a regular at several dive bars within walking distance of her apartment on Stanton Street—the grungier, the better.

The hipster haunt of the greatest Gaga lore would be St. Jerome's (155 Rivington Street), where she met her earliest muse, Lüc Carl, slinging flat beers behind the bar. The aspiring rocker was a tall glass of whiskey, dressed in leather and spandex with a bandanna taming his 1980s-era signature hairdo. As manager of St. Jerome's for five years, Lüc was also in charge of entertainment and gave Gaga her start as a go-go dancer. The two dated on and off for six years until 2011, their romantic saga immortalized in "Yoü and I," with lyrics reminiscing about their good times at St. Jerome's.

Just a short stumble down the block from St. Jerome's (which closed in 2012), Welcome to the Johnsons at 123 Rivington is furnished to resemble a 1970s basement with wood-paneled walls, Little League trophies, and vintage sofas covered in protective plastic. But it's not your grandmother's dive bar, it's Gaga's—and she's returned to Welcome to the Johnsons many times since becoming famous.

She returned to her roots in 2016 for the Dive Bar Tour, a three-show trek to promote *Joanne* sponsored by Bud Light. The second stop was a place where Gaga performed as an unsigned act: the Bitter End, New York's oldest rock club, located in Greenwich Village. "I've been playing here since I was fifteen years old," she told the crowd. "This is where I started."

ENIGMA + JAZZ & PIANO

Since 2018, Mother Monster has entertained audiences in Las Vegas with Enigma + Jazz & Piano, her concert residency at the Park MGM casino. They're two types of shows: Enigma features stripped-down versions of her greatest hits, while Jazz & Piano is exactly that, a set list of Great American Songbook standards backed by a thirty-piece band. Each production also has its own theme, wardrobe, and stage decor. Enigma, which is based on Gaga's *Artpop*-era alter ego Petga, is set in a postapocalyptic punk virtual world with sci-fi costumes made of metallic fabrics, latex, and leather, while Jazz & Piano channels Old Hollywood glamour with sequins, rhinestones, feathers, tassels, and even a champagne-colored gown adorned with fifty-three thousand Swarovski crystals.

For Little Monsters, Enigma's set list runs through Gaga's discography, beginning with her first single, "Just Dance," through *Born This Way*'s "Edge of Glory" and "Judas," *Artpop*'s "Applause," *Joanne* standout "Million Reasons," and the finale, "Shallow," from *A Star Is Born*. Jazz & Piano, Gaga's more popular show, is many of the same classics from her Tony Bennett collaborations, including "The Lady Is a Tramp," "Cheek to Cheek," and "Let's Face the Music and Dance."

Gaga reportedly signed a $100 million deal for Enigma + Jazz & Piano, the highest-grossing Vegas concert residency in 2019. Jazz & Piano also enjoyed an eight-night run in summer 2024.

FRENCH BULLDOGS

Mother Monster is a dedicated dog mama to her three French bulldogs, Asia, Gustav, and Koji. The "three little piggies," as Gaga calls them, go just about everywhere with their famous owner, from award shows to world tours, and always travel aboard her private plane. The eldest of the pack is Asia, a gift to Gaga from her then-fiancé, Taylor Kinney, in 2014, and the following year made history as the first face of the Coach Pups Campaign. She's also the only one of the three dogs who has her own Instagram account, @MissAsiaXOXO. Not long after Asia's first birthday, the pup introduced her new little brother Koji to her 210,000 followers: "His name

MOTHER MONSTER IS A DEDICATED DOG MAMA TO HER THREE FRENCH BULLDOGS, ASIA, GUSTAV, AND KOJI.

means 'little one' because he is so small!'" In 2016, Gaga welcomed a third French into the family, Gustav, who she also refers to as "cowpig" and "moopig" due to his white-and-black coloring.

In 2021, while in Italy filming *House of Gucci*, Gaga left Asia, Koji, and Gustav in the trusted care of their dog walker, Ryan Fischer, in Los Angeles. One night while out on a walk, a group of men spotted Fischer with the expensive pups and held him at gunpoint, demanding he hand over the leashes. He bravely fought back and was shot once in the chest, as the men grabbed Koji and Gustav and fled (Asia hid under nearby bushes). Fischer was rushed to the hospital, where he underwent emergency surgery. "You risked your life to fight for our family. You're forever a hero," said Gaga, who offered a $500,000 reward for Koji and Gustav's safe return. Two days later, the dogs were recovered and a total of five people were arrested and charged with a range of crimes, including the gunman, who was sentenced to twenty-one years in prison.

THERE IS NO "I" IN LADY GAGA.

GUINNESS WORLD RECORDS

Since 2009, Lady Gaga has set at least fourteen Guinness World
Records, for everything from singles sales and Grammy wins to product
placements in a video. The first year of her career, the "Just Dance"
singer was recognized as the Most Downloaded Female Act in a Year with
11.1 million in the United States. In 2010—the year she took the title of
Most Searched-For Female on the Internet—Gaga also received the most
MTV Video Music Awards nominations in a single year (thirteen) and
"Telephone" featured the most product placements in a music video with
more than a dozen, including Chanel, Wonder Bread, Diet Coke, Polaroid,
Kraft's Miracle Whip, and Virgin Mobile.

Gaga's second studio album, *Born This Way*, was the fastest-selling US
digital album of 2011, and its lead single of the same name was the year's

fastest-selling single on iTunes—a record that has since been broken by Taylor Swift's "We Are Never Getting Back Together." Between 2007 and 2016, Gaga had the most-viewed Wikipedia page (80 million) of all women and female musicians, trailing only President Barack Obama and Michael Jackson of all people. One of the most decorated of her generation, the double threat became the first person ever to be nominated for Best Actress (*A Star Is Born*) and Best Original Song ("Shallow") at the Academy Awards in one year (2019).

HAUS OF GAGA

There is no "I" in Lady Gaga—it takes a team of artistic professionals to bring her innovative visions to life. Known as Haus of Gaga, the collective of creatives are primarily responsible for cultivating her image both on and off the stage, from red carpet fashion and glam to tour costumes, sets, and performances. "It's a real bond and relationship, and that's what I think music and art is about," the singer explained to MTV News in 2009. "They are my heart and soul. They believe in me, and they look at me like a mother and daughter and sister, with pride and love."

Modeled after Andy Warhol's Factory, the Haus of Gaga takes its name from Bauhaus, the German artistic movement of the 1920s and '30s that intended to unify all the arts. In the Gagaverse, there's regular crossover between team members to elevate her ideas: a makeup artist and prop studio creating a lipstick gun for the "Judas" music video; her hairstylist inventing a fiber-optic wig to be controlled by her lighting designer during shows; and collaborations between fashion and tech departments, like the time Gaga rode a half-human horse made of recycled Chanel purses onto the red carpet at the 2013 American Music Awards.

Two of the longest running members of the Haus of Gaga are hairstylist Frederic Aspiras and makeup artist Sarah Tanno, who have been with Mother Monster since 2009 and worked on every single tour, music video, and awards show, as well as *A Star Is Born* and *House of Gucci*. "It's nice to know you have people around you that you have known for a long time that you trust and that you believe in and that they believe in you," Aspiras told *People*. "We have this long history of this amazing body of work that we're so proud of, and there's a lot more to do." Tanno—who married fellow Haus of Gaga member, touring guitarist Tim Stewart, in 2019—echoed Aspiras in the same interview: "Our aesthetic of what we think is beautiful is very similar, which is why we work so well together."

INAUGURATION

Lady Gaga rang in a new era for America on January 20, 2021, when she performed the national anthem at President Joe Biden's inauguration; she described it as "the honor of my lifetime" to *People*. She sounded flawless—and looked it, too, in a Schiaparelli haute couture design that stayed true to the singer's avant-garde grandeur, with a patriotic twist: a voluminous, red silk faille skirt and fitted navy cashmere jacket accessorized with a gilded dove of peace brooch over her heart.

It would be another ten months before she revealed the most important detail of her custom gown that no one noticed at the time: "There was a bulletproof vest sewn into the dress," Gaga told *Vogue*. Only two weeks after far-right extremists stormed the US Capitol in opposition of Biden's election, "It was a scary time in this country," she acknowledged. "I care a lot about my family. As a performer, I understand that I put myself in all types of dangerous situations in order to do what

I love. And so I did that for myself, but for my family, as well, so that my mom and dad and my sister would feel confident."

Gaga's outfit wasn't the only viral moment during her inauguration performance—the internet swooned over the Marine who escorted her down the stairs to the podium. Right before she walked out to the Capitol's West Front, there was last-minute concern she might trip on her voluminous skirt. "So they basically looked around and I was one of the taller, larger individuals, and they just asked if I would be willing to assist and I was more than happy to," Capt. Evan Campbell told *Task and Purpose*. As they waited in the wings, he could tell Gaga was nervous and the two prayed together before heading toward the podium. "I was truly impressed with how genuine she was," praised Capt. Campbell, who admittedly became a Little Monster that day.

JOANNE TRATTORIA

The Germanottas serve up family recipes at their Southern Italian restaurant on the Upper West Side, named after Gaga's paternal aunt who died from lupus a decade before the pop star was born. Opened in 2012 by Joe and Cynthia, Joanne's menu was created by Art Smith, Oprah's former personal chef. Popular dishes include Big Joe's Eggplant Parm, Papa G's Chicken Scarpariello, and Joanne's Meatballs, as well as plenty of vegetarian and vegan options.

The cozy eatery, located on West 68th Street, just a few streets away from where Gaga grew up, is meant to feel like home for diners, with family photos lining the walls. In the spirit of Gaga, Joanne's offers regular live entertainment from singers, jazz trios, and on Wednesdays, a free drag show dubbed Drag Me to Joanne's, hosted by Jupiter Genesis.

"I WAS TRULY IMPRESSED
WITH HOW GENUINE SHE WAS."

KOONS

Gaga introduced Little Monsters to one of her all-time favorite artists
in "Applause," the first single off *Artpop*. Jeff Koons is best known for
his sculptures of everyday objects, most famously balloon animals done
in multicolored, mirror-polished stainless steel ("Rabbit" sold for
$91.1 million in 2019).

Gaga was a longtime admirer of the artist's work when she got the
chance to meet him at the 2010 MET Gala following her performance. "She
just kind of grabbed ahold of me and gave me a big hug around my waist
and she just said, 'You know, Jeff, I've been such a fan of yours, and when I
was a kid just hanging out in Central Park I would talk to my friends about
your work,'" he recalled to MTV News. Three years later, Gaga asked the
artist to sculpt her for the cover of *Artpop*.

GAGA'S FAN BASE HAS THEIR VERY OWN DIGITAL CLUBHOUSE, CREATED BY MOTHER MONSTER HERSELF.

The sixteen-foot (5 m) white plaster replica of Gaga, nude and cupping her breasts, with a blue gazing ball between her legs, was displayed at the two-day ArtRave in New York to promote the album. The gazing ball, which was also incorporated into a costume for the Artpop Ball, is a symbol of "this aspect of reflection that when you come across something like a gazing ball, it affirms you, it affirms your existence and then from that affirmation, you start to want more," Koons explained to MTV. "There's a transcendence that takes place and eventually it really leads you to everything."

LITTLEMONSTERS.COM

Gaga's fan base has their very own digital clubhouse, created by Mother
Monster herself: LittleMonsters.com. Launched in 2012, the website and
app make up a social network connecting people all over the world through
the power of Gaga. Members can join groups and chat with other Little
Monsters, share content, watch videos, listen to music, purchase concert
tickets, and shop merchandise.

The singer came up with the idea in 2010, after seeing *The Social
Network*, a film about the founding of Facebook. She left the theater and
called her then-business manager Troy Carter, who assembled a team of
engineers who worked seven days a week to develop Mother Monster's idea
(with $19 million in funding, including her own $1 million investment).
Less than a year later, LittleMonsters.com launched an invite-only beta
phase with fifty thousand members. Within a year of opening to the
public, the fan community had grown to a million. In the early days, Gaga
contributed regularly, as did Haus of Gaga–verified members like her
stylist Nicola Formichetti, makeup artist Tara Savelo, and music producer
Fernando Garibay.

In 2016, the company that built the site and app ran out of money,
yet LittleMonsters.com has continued to hobble along with low-tech
features. Today, its popularity has waned considerably thanks to Instagram
and TikTok.

MANIFESTOS

Gaga has made more than one public declaration celebrating her
dedicated fan base. The first, "Manifesto of Little Monsters," debuted
during the Monster Ball Tour, a black-and-white video interlude between

segments narrated by Mother Monster. "The real truth about Lady Gaga fans lies in this sentiment: They are the kings. They are the queens. They write the history of the kingdom, while I am something of a devoted Jester," she said. On page 5 of the *Book of Gaga*, included in *The Fame Monster* box set, the "Manifesto of Little Monsters" is typed out and signed by their fearless leader with the closing, "When you're lonely, I'll be lonely too."

Two years later, Gaga traced the fictional origins of Little Monsters in the "Manifesto of Mother Monster," revealing that she gave birth to them in space on G.O.A.T. (Government Owned Alien Territory). As she explains, "the new race" of Monsters bears no prejudice or judgment, but the same day they entered the multiverse, so did evil. Mother Monster brought her manifesto to life in the "Born This Way" video, which opens with a visual depiction of the "birth of magnificent and magical proportions," a dramatic scene scored by the musical prelude of Alfred Hitchcock's 1958 thriller *Vertigo*.

NURTEC

Since her teens, Gaga has suffered from debilitating migraines so extreme she would have to miss school as she spent days in bed in a darkened room until the pain subsided. As an adult, she found relief with Nurtec ODT, a prescription medication, but her partnership with pharmaceutical giant Pfizer gave fans a headache. Gaga's first Nurtec commercial debuted in June 2023, during Migraine and Headache Awareness Month, showing the singer performing on the Chromatica Ball Tour while explaining the medication's benefits in voice-over. She also posted a sponsored ad on

Instagram listing the side effects, which didn't sit right with many of her fifty-five million followers, who flooded the comments section with replies like, "Less Lady Pharma, more Lady Gaga."

Despite the online backlash, Nurtec dropped a second commercial with Gaga in April 2024, directed by fashion photography duo Inez van Lamsweerde and Vinoodh Matadin. "Nothing dims my light like a migraine," the singer says as she gets glam for a photo shoot. "To those with migraines, I see you. It's time we all shine."

OLYMPICS

Oh là là! Gaga took home the gold at the Paris 2024 Olympics opening ceremony with her performance of "Mon Truc En Plumes" ("My Thing With Feathers"), a 1960s French cabaret classic by ballet dancer-actress Zizi Jeanmaire. With a golden staircase along the River Seine as her stage, the American superstar strutted her stuff in a black Dior Haute Couture ensemble, accompanied by a dozen dancers shaking bubblegum-pink pom-poms and feather fans. The choreographed spectacle—featuring an interlude of Gaga playing piano—was an ode to Jeanmaire's 1965 appearance on American variety show *The Ed Sullivan Show.*

"I wanted nothing more than to create a performance that would warm the heart of France, celebrate French art and music, and on such a momentous occasion remind everyone of one of the most magical cities on earth—Paris," Gaga wrote on Instagram. "And to everyone in France, thank you so much for welcoming me to your country to sing in honor of you—it's a gift I'll never forget!"

WHAT'S A STAGE PERFORMANCE WITHOUT A LITTLE PYRO?

PYROTECHNIC BRA

What's a stage performance without a little pyro? Gaga's debut at the 2009 Much Music Video Awards was lit—literally, beginning with the singer blowing up a subway car with a stick of dynamite to sparks shooting from her studded leather bustier during the final note of "Poker Face." The custom-made metal Pyro Bra operated via a remote in Gaga's hand that triggered two miniature motors with carbide grinding wheels to spin. Another button pushed a piece of steel into the wheels, acting as a flint. Looking back on the iconic fashion statement a decade later with *Vogue*, she revealed that originally, "I wanted it to shoot fire from my breasts, but we decided it was safer to shoot sparks."

LADY GAGA IS DERIVED FROM QUEEN'S 1984 SONG "RADIO GA GA."

The too-hot-for-TV moment made headlines the next morning, just as Gaga's stylist Nicola Formichetti was making his way through security at Toronto Pearson International Airport with the flammable costume. "They opened my suitcase and, basically, it looked like I had a bomb," Formichetti recalled to the *Globe and Mail*. "I thought they were going to put me in prison when, by chance, a guy walked past and said, 'Oh my god, that's Gaga's bra from last night!' Then they all started laughing and let me go."

The Pyro Bra was a staple of the Monster Ball Tour and even made an appearance on the 2010 cover of *Time* 100, which Gaga shared with former president Bill Clinton and Apple CEO Steve Jobs.

QUEEN

The British rock band fronted by showman Freddie Mercury inspired Stefani Germanotta's stage name. Lady Gaga is derived from Queen's 1984 song "Radio Ga Ga," about television becoming more popular than radio in the 1950s, and then music videos and the advent of MTV doing the same three decades later. "The visual side seems to be almost more important," explained the song's writer, Queen drummer Roger Taylor. Music as performance art became Lady Gaga's persona, but years earlier, as Stefani, the young singer evoked Mercury's vocal gymnastics in the recording studio with her first producer, Rob Fusari, who coined the nickname Lady Gaga as a joke. It stuck.

In one of her earliest interviews, Gaga explained her love of Queen, a band her father introduced her to as a kid. "It's theatrical, it's opera, it's pop, it's rock, it's all the things that I try to implement into my show," she told French radio station NRJ. In 2011, she had a full-circle moment on her second studio album, when Queen guitarist Brian May agreed to play on arena-rock power ballad "Yoü and I." Upon hearing the news, "I fell to the floor crying and laughing," Gaga told *The Sun*. The rock legend was just as honored to collaborate with her—and considered her a worthy replacement for the late Mercury for Queen's 2012 tour. Unfortunately, Gaga was already booked for the Born This Way Ball, and the band signed *American Idol* finalist Adam Lambert, who has been Queen's front man ever since.

ROMANCES (GOOD, BAD, AND OTHERWISE)

Much of Gaga's early music was inspired by her relationship with bartender-musician Lüc Carl, whom she met in 2005 and dated on and off for six years. She sang about her obsession with him on "Paparazzi"

and their rekindled love on "Yoü and I," but he became her betrayer in "Judas." When the two split the first time in 2009, Gaga mixed pleasure with business, courting Matthew Williams, creative director of Haus of Gaga. "We were crazy lovers, but I stopped it when we discovered what a strong creative connection we had," she confessed to the *Evening Standard* in 2010.

Life imitated art when Gaga fell for Taylor Kinney, who portrayed her love interest in the "Yoü and I" video. The chemistry was palpable, and after the shoot, he and Gaga exchanged numbers. Still, it was another two years before the private relationship went public, when Gaga and Taylor walked the red carpet at the 2014 Golden Globes. "He's the first man that I have dated that, when I sing onstage, he cries," she told the *Times*. "That means more to me than anything."

On Valentine's Day 2015, Taylor proposed with a heart-shaped diamond ring, but the wedding planning didn't get very far. As chronicled in her documentary *Five Foot Two*, the couple was already on the rocks when Gaga's casting in *A Star Is Born* put the final nail in the coffin. In July 2016, Gaga announced the "soulmates" were taking a break from their five-year relationship.

The following year, Gaga found new love with Hollywood talent agent Christian Carino, who was by her side as Gaga performed on the biggest stage in music, the Super Bowl Halftime Show, in 2017. Within months, he popped the question with a pink sapphire and diamond cluster ring, but once again the singer didn't make it down the aisle: she and Christian split in February 2019.

Gaga rang in new romance on New Year's Eve 2020 with tech entrepreneur Michael Polansky. Three months later, the relationship was tested by the COVID-19 lockdown—and proved they could collaborate professionally. The Harvard grad helped his girlfriend organize *Together at Home*, a benefit concert that raised $128 million for health care workers. In fall 2022, it was reported the couple was "taking some breathing space"—but in April 2024, Gaga was photographed with a massive diamond on her ring finger. Three months later, she unofficially confirmed the engagement news at the Paris Olympics when she introduced Michael as "my fiancé" to French Prime Minister Gabriel Attal.

SUPER BOWL HALFTIME SHOW

A year after singing the national anthem at the Super Bowl, Gaga returned to headline the 2017 Halftime Show—and she kicked off her historic performance from the roof of the NRG Stadium in Houston, Texas. Standing more than two hundred feet (60 m) in the air, the singer opened with a medley of "God Bless America," "This Land Is Your Land," and the Pledge of Allegiance, as hundreds of red, white, and blue drones formed the American flag in the night sky behind her. It had always been Gaga's vision to dive from the roof down to the stage below, but safety concerns, logistics, and unpredictable winter weather prevented her from doing it live, and the segment was pretaped. But it was certainly the real deal as Gaga descended ninety feet (27 m) from the darkness down to a massive tower, where she launched right into "Poker Face." A harness attached to her Atelier Versace iridescent bodysuit then catapulted her up into the air, so she could backflip another forty feet (12 m) down to the stage.

Following a dance number to "Born This Way," "Telephone," and "Just Dance," Gaga made her way over to a smaller second stage shaped like a plant of shining light (with a beating heart at its center) for a piano

A RECORD 5.6 PERCENT MORE PEOPLE TUNED IN TO WATCH GAGA THAN THE ACTUAL GAME, A TOTAL OF 117.5 MILLION TELEVISION VIEWERS.

interlude of "Million Reasons." The final set gave a nod to the NFL: Gaga and her dancers, all clad in bedazzled shoulder pads and helmets, performed "Bad Romance." As if she'd made the winning play, the dancers carried Gaga on their shoulders to a side stage, where she caught a touchdown (thrown by an actual quarterback) and jumped out of frame.

A record 5.6 percent more people tuned in to watch Gaga than the actual game, a total of 117.5 million television viewers, the fourth most of all time behind Usher, Rihanna, and Katy Perry. Critics agreed Mother Monster's performance was "one of the best halftime sets of the century" and it received six Primetime Creative Arts Emmy nominations, the most of any halftime show.

"THERE IS NOBODY MORE BADASS THAN TONY BENNETT."

TONY BENNETT

When Gaga felt like the whole industry turned its back on her following the perceived failure of *Artpop*, one person was there to help her move forward: Tony Bennett. At nearly ninety, the jazz singer may have seemed like an unlikely friend, but the five decades between them was nothing but a number. "There is nobody more badass than Tony Bennett," Gaga told *Billboard* in 2015, a year after their first collaboration, *Cheek to Cheek*, which debuted at No. 1 on the *Billboard* 200 chart. "That man is a part of the history of music in a way that is extremely powerful, and he taught me to stay true to who I am, to not let anybody exploit me."

Bennett was diagnosed with Alzheimer's in 2015, and as he prepared to close the curtain on a legendary career, he ended on a high note: one last album with Lady Gaga, 2021's *Love for Sale*. Bennett's final performance was a two-night engagement at New York's Radio City Music Hall, which was recorded for a CBS prime-time special, *One Last Time: An Evening with Tony Bennett and Lady Gaga*. At the 2022 Grammy Awards, *Love for Sale* won Best Traditional Pop Vocal Album, and although Bennett was not well enough to attend the ceremony, Gaga made sure he felt the love. She performed solo versions of their duets in a medley as a video montage played in the background. "I love you Tony, we miss you," she told him from the stage.

The following July, Bennett died, just shy of his ninety-seventh birthday. Gaga remembered her "true friend" on Instagram with a photo of the two embracing and a lengthy caption describing their timeless bond. "Tony and I had this magical power. We transported ourselves to another era, modernized the music together, and gave it all new life as a singing duo . . . I'll never forget this experience. I'll never forget Tony Bennett."

UNICORNS

From one magical creature to another, Gaga's love of unicorns is not a myth! During the *Born This Way* era, she featured the fantastical creature—which symbolizes purity and strength—on the album's track list ("Highway Unicorn") and in the music video for "Born This Way." For her world tour, Haus of Gaga customized a life-size fiberglass Unicorn Piano with a purple spire, a two-tone black and blonde tail, and a shelf in its torso for her eighty-eight keys. Jim Henson's Creature Shop also created the human-operated unicorn puppet Gaga rode onstage, which was later repainted white for her grand entrance at the 2013 American Music Awards.

The singer—who has a unicorn tattoo on her left thigh—even wore Noritaka Tatehana's "Unicorn" boots, towering heelless shoes with a golden horn on the tip. Gaga is such a fan of the Japanese designer that she owns more than twenty pairs of his traditional Geisha-inspired shoes with sculptural platforms, which range in height from ten to eighteen inches (25 to 46 cm) and sell for $15,000 each.

VERY GAGA THANKSGIVING

Mother Monster started a new holiday tradition for her fans with *A Very Gaga Thanksgiving*, a prime-time television special that aired on ABC in November 2011. The ninety-minute holiday program combined intimate performances and a sit-down interview with Katie Couric, all shot at her alma mater, the Convent of the Sacred Heart.

ABC promised "a chance to see more of who she is beneath the wild costumes and staged musical numbers"—and that's exactly what Little Monsters got, in several wonderfully wacky segments. In one, Gaga makes glittery Thanksgiving crafts with a group of third-graders. Later, she whips up modern takes on family recipes like fried turkey and Grandmother Germanotta's Salami-Pecorino Cheese Waffles, all while dressed in Valentino couture. During a piano rendition of "Hair" in a candlelit room, she stops several times to pile different wigs on top of her head, including one that's teal, a color that represents bullying prevention awareness, for all the kids "who are afraid to be themselves." There's even a touching moment when one of the Sacred Heart nuns surprises her most famous pupil to share stories about little Stefani Germanotta.

Nearly six million people tuned in for *A Very Gaga Thanksgiving*, ABC's best ratings in four years. A four-song EP of select performances, including jazz covers of Irving Berlin's 1942 classic "White Christmas" and Nat King Cole's "Orange Colored Sky," was simultaneously released as *A Very Gaga Holiday*.

WEDNESDAY ADDAMS

Of course, Wednesday Addams would be a Little Monster. The pigtailed gothic icon from *The Addams Family* franchise resurrected "Bloody Mary," a deep cut from *Born This Way*, eleven years later. It all began with a viral clip from *Wednesday* of the titular character (Jenna Ortega) dancing to the Cramps' 1981 song "Goo Goo Muck" on the Netflix series. As fans around the world recreated the kooky choreography on TikTok, one genius Little Monster replaced the audio with a sped-up version of "Bloody Mary"—and the result was altogether ooky.

Streams of the song spiked 509 percent, as "Bloody Mary" climbed *Billboard*'s Adult Top 40 chart to No. 3. Gaga's record label also released "Bloody Mary" on vinyl, with a glow-in-the-dark special edition pressed just for Halloween 2023. Wednesday proved misery really does love company when the fictional character tweeted about Gaga, "I understand she is followed by little monsters. I approve." Mother Monster responded with her own "Bloody Mary" dance video as well as a personal invitation to Wednesday: "You're welcome at Haus of Gaga anytime (and bring Thing with you, we love paws around here)."

X LADY GAGA

In music, Gaga has collaborated with artists from nearly every genre—Beyoncé, Ariana Grande, Tony Bennett, Metallica, Rolling Stones—and in business, her portfolio is just as diverse. In 2009, following

"YOU'RE WELCOME AT HAUS OF GAGA ANYTIME (AND BRING THING WITH YOU, WE LOVE PAWS AROUND HERE)."

the billion-dollar success of Beats by Dre headphones, Monster Cable next partnered with the "Poker Face" singer on Heartbeats by Lady Gaga, jewel-encrusted earbuds designed to look like earrings that made cameos in music videos for "Bad Romance" and "Telephone." Next, as a creative director at Polaroid, she developed her own Grey Label product line with the Haus of Gaga that included a digital camera and mobile printer for smartphone images.

During the *Born This Way* era, the singer celebrated her holiday-themed Gaga's Workshop at Barney's New York with more than two hundred custom collectibles, like plush Little Monsters, teacup-and-saucer sets, lace sunglasses, a stiletto stocking, a snow globe,

"IMMERSIVE EXPERIENCES WITH ART I THINK REALLY LEAVE AN IMPRINT ON THE SOUL."

and a motorcycle jacket. To promote *Chromatica*, Little Monsters were treated to Oreo x Lady Gaga, a limited-edition release that transformed the iconic black-and-white cookies into pink wafers with green creme filling. Fans over twenty-one could wash it down with Dom Perignon x Lady Gaga, exclusive champagnes that retailed between $249 and $439.

Gaga tapped into the gaming industry in 2024 as the featured performer in Fortnite Festival, which allows players to live out their rock-star fantasies. With the Fortnite x Lady Gaga collaboration, players can unlock several of the Chromatica Ball's costumes and instruments. "Immersive experiences with art I think really leave an imprint on the soul," she wrote on Instagram, "and it changes the texture of how we experience pop culture."

YELLOW WIG

A natural brunette who went blonde for *The Fame*, Gaga has used wigs to experiment further with hair color: lavender, pink, aqua, teal, orange, and what she calls "piss yellow." In pop art, particularly the work of Roy Lichtenstein, blondes are represented with yellow hair, which inspired Gaga's hairstylist-wigmaker Frederic Aspiras for the Monster Ball Tour in 2009.

A decade later, Gaga recalled the moment of genius at the annual Fashion Los Angeles Awards, where she honored Aspiras with Hairstylist of the Year. "As I was sitting in the glam chair, slowly his hand ripped out a page from Italian *Vogue* across the table with a model who had piss-yellow hair," she related. "I said, 'Freddie, what is that?' He said, 'I know, I was just thinking.' And then he stopped talking. I said, 'Freddie, with this hair and with this makeup, I would look like a live Lichtenstein.' He said, 'Yes.' I said, 'This is live pop art.'"

The first "piss-yellow" wig had an extra edge with dark roots, and evolved in style and hue over the Monsters Ball. For Gaga's first Grammy Awards in 2010, when the rookie was up for five golden gramophones, Aspiras created a more elegant version with lighter roots to complement her cosmic lavender Armani wardrobe with cylindrical orbiting rings.

ZAPPA HOUSE

Gaga purchased a piece of rock history in 2016, when she snapped up Frank Zappa's quirky Los Angeles compound, where the experimental musician lived and worked for the last two decades of his life. Located in Laurel Canyon, the seven-bedroom Tudor mansion and its two guest cottages are an artist's dream, a combination of utility and whimsy

featuring a recording studio, climate-controlled vault, double-height art gallery, steampunk spiral staircase, murals and mosaics, rooftop tennis court, library floor painted to look like a lily pond, and porthole windows and doors salvaged from vintage submarines.

But for Gaga, the eccentric estate of "intricate chaos" was not a home, but a workspace. Her primary residence continued to be a $23 million cliffside Mediterranean villa in Malibu, while the $5.25 million woodland hideaway was where she painted, wrote songs (she literally scribbled lyrics in black Sharpie on a white piano), and planned out her Las Vegas residency with her creative team. Inside the "Utility Muffin Research Kitchen"—Zappa's nickname for the studio where he made a whopping sixty albums—Gaga recorded several tracks for *A Star Is Born*'s soundtrack and *Chromatica*. The Zappa House also doubled as an art museum to exhibit her many pop culture artifacts, like Michael Jackson's "Bad" jacket and crystal glove, as well as her own memorabilia: a fifteen-foot (4.5 m) framed photograph of her face in the final scene of *A Star Is Born*, a gift from Bradley Cooper.

After five years, Gaga sold the Zappa House to someone with their own rock heritage: Mick Jagger's daughter Elizabeth paid $6.45 million in an off-market deal in 2021.

PART FOUR

Mother Monster

DON'T BE A DRAG

Before Gaga was a pop icon, she was already a gay icon. In August 2008, two months before *The Fame* was unleashed on an unsuspecting world, a baby-faced singer named Lady Gaga performed a three-song set at the San Francisco Pride festival. The stage was her biggest to date, with 1.2 million in attendance as she and two awkward backup dancers worked through "LoveGame" and "Beautiful, Dirty, Rich." And then came the opening synth notes of "Just Dance." It would be weeks before the single even entered the *Billboard* Hot 100 chart, yet the crowd seemed to know every word, singing the song even after the music ended.

A year later, as *The Fame* surpassed the five-million mark in sales, Gaga looked back at the impact of San Francisco Pride. "Being invited to play, that was a real turning point for me as an artist," she told MTV News. "I've got so many gay fans and they're so loyal to me and they really lifted me up. They'll always stand by me and I'll always stand by them."

And that wasn't lip service. Gaga has been a tireless advocate for the LGBTQ+ community, whether she's fighting for equal rights, exposing homophobic propaganda around the world, or simply talking about how much the community means to her. She dedicated one of her first awards, International Video of the Year at the 2009 Much Music Video Awards, "to God and the gays." That same year, in a now famous interview, Gaga leveraged her devoted fan base to shut down a reporter badgering her about sexual references in her music. When he asked about the biggest thrill of her career thus far, she quipped, "The gay community. 'Cause I love them so much. 'Cause they don't ask me questions like that. 'Cause they love sexual, strong women who speak their mind."

One of Gaga's earliest shows of activism was in opposition to "Don't ask, don't tell," the official US policy that barred openly gay, lesbian, or bisexual people from military service. President Barack Obama had pledged a full repeal of DADT during his campaign, yet once in office he provided only a vague timetable for its removal. Gaga was vocal in her disappointment, demanding immediate action at the 2009 National Equality March in Washington, DC. On the Capitol Building's West Lawn, she stood before tens of thousands—some holding signs reading "Gay for Gaga" and "Lady Gaga [heart] Equality, U Should 2"—and called out the president's inaction.

"Are you listening?" she demanded. "We will continue to push your administration to bring your promise to reality . . . I will never turn my

GAGA HAS BEEN
A TIRELESS ADVOCATE
FOR THE LGBTQ+ COMMUNITY.

back on my friends. Today is not a one-off performance." A year later, when the Obama administration still hadn't done anything about DADT, Gaga took advantage of her global platform at the 2010 Video Music Awards as the show's most-nominated artist in history. With all eyes on her, the "Paparazzi" singer walked the red carpet with four members of the US military who were no longer serving due to the discriminatory policy—which Obama finally repealed in September 2011.

That same year, Gaga gifted her devoted fan base their very own anthem with "Born This Way," which encourages people of all sexual orientations, genders, ages, and races to accept themselves and reject prejudices. It made history as the first No. 1 song to contain "transgender" in its lyrics. Six years later, when she performed the track during the Super Bowl Halftime Show, she became the first person to ever say the words "lesbian," "gay," "bi," or "transgender" in a Super Bowl broadcast.

With her *Born This Way* album, the singer hoped to reform one of the largest retail chains in the country. During negotiations with Target to exclusively partner for a special edition, Gaga requested the company—which had donated to an anti-gay political action committee—"start affiliating themselves with LGBT charity groups," she told *Billboard*. "Our relationship is hinged upon their reform in the company to support the gay community." When talks went nowhere, Gaga dissolved her association with Target, a financial sacrifice that proved her integrity as an advocate.

She didn't just fight for gay Americans. In 2012, the same year she pushed for marriage equality in the US, the singer risked her own freedom for inclusivity in Russia. In St. Petersburg, where gay "propaganda" is banned, Gaga was threatened with arrest if her tour, Born This Way Ball, went on as scheduled. But she wouldn't back down. "Tonight, this is my house, Russia," she declared from the stage in December 2012. "You can be gay in my house."

For every win, there was a loss—and the bisexual singer grieved tragedy along with the community. On June 12, 2016, a gunman opened fire at Pulse, a gay nightclub in Orlando, Florida, killing forty-nine people, the deadliest mass shooting in US history at the time. At a rally in Los Angeles, a makeup-free Gaga tearfully eulogized "these innocent, beautiful people . . . They are sons and daughters. They were fathers and mothers. They are all our brothers and our sisters." Speaking directly to the gay community, she continued, "I hope you know that myself and so many are your allies. We represent the compassion and the loyalty of millions of people around the world that believe in you. You are not alone—you are *not* alone."

In 2018, in a moment of true pride and joy, Gaga fooled some of the most famous drag queens on Season 9 of *RuPaul's Drag Race*. She strutted onto set as Ronnie, "New Jersey's #1 Lady Gaga impersonator"—until she opened her mouth to announce, "Mother Monster has arrived." Once the shock wore off, there wasn't a dry eye in the house as queen Eureka took the opportunity to tell Gaga about her life-changing influence. "I've been the closest to death, and you've pulled me out of it," she said. "You don't realize what you do for people, and how much you inspire people like me and all of us. You allow us to be who we are."

Even as one of the best-selling musical artists, Gaga has never forgotten her roots. Over the years, Gaga has regularly celebrated at Pride parades. In 2019, she made a surprise appearance at Stonewall in New York City for the fiftieth anniversary of the bar's 1969 uprising, during which patrons fought back against a discriminatory police raid. "This is my mothership, and you are my leaders and I will follow you," vowed the singer, decked out in thigh-high glittery rainbow boots. "True love is when you would take a bullet for someone, and you know that I would take a bullet for you any day of the week."

A decade after *Born This Way*, she celebrated its impact with a special-edition album of additional remixes and covers by LGBTQ+ artists and allies. In West Hollywood, the first majority-gay municipality in the US, May 23, 2021, was officially declared Born This Way Day, and Gaga was honored with the keys to the city. "Through her music and activism, Lady Gaga has become a cultural icon for our generation," said Mayor Lindsey P. Horvath. "The anthem 'Born This Way' has become an out-and-proud declarative stance for countless LGBTQ people . . . Thank you for encouraging us to love ourselves and be proud!"

The feeling was mutual, insisted an emotional Gaga. "Thank you so much for showing me what it means to be brave," she told the crowd gathered outside the Abbey, a world-famous and historic gay bar. "I'm sure this will sound cheesy to some people, but not to me—you've been the motherfucking key to my heart for a long time."

STYLE AND SUBSTANCE

For a performance artist like Lady Gaga, music and fashion go together like Andy Warhol and a can of Campbell's soup. That creative intersection had been dormant in pop culture until she arrived in 2008. "When I'm writing music, I'm thinking about the clothes I want to wear on stage," she told MTV News at the time. "It's all about everything all together—performance art, pop performance art, fashion. For me, it's everything coming together and being a real story that will bring back the superfan . . . I want the imagery to be so strong that fans will want to eat and taste and lick every part of us."

"I JUST KNEW
I HAD TO BLEED TO DEATH
FOR FOUR MINUTES ON TV.""

But her dramatic flair isn't purely for shock value. Many of Gaga's most iconic looks symbolize something far greater, conveying a message through latex, fishnets, studded leather, and even strips of raw meat.

THERE WILL BE BLOOD
Going into the 2009 MTV Video Music Awards, Gaga was tied with Beyoncé for most nominations, with nine apiece. However, the battle between the world's two biggest pop stars became merely a footnote in the pop culture history books—and not just because Kanye West would interrupt Taylor Swift's acceptance speech later in the evening. First, Gaga stole the show with her performance of "Paparazzi," a spectacle of blood, bedazzled wheelchairs, and medical bandage fashion.

From the moment the curtain rose on the *Phantom of the Opera*esque set, it promised to be memorable. The singer, lying on the ground beside a fallen chandelier, ad-libs the line, "Amidst all of these flashing lights, I pray the fame won't take my life." By the end of the performance, she doesn't get her wish. After a piano interlude that has her pounding on the keys, one leg up on the instrument, Gaga stands and turns to the audience, a noticeable red stain spreading across her white lace bodysuit. She stumbles, everyone gasps—is this part of the act? But Gaga continues to sing as fake blood gushes down her torso. Backup dancers appear to come to her rescue, but then she screams out in pain. The graphic scene culminates with her limp body rising over the stage, her face smeared in blood, eyes glazed over in death.

The performance had everyone talking, even if no one was quite sure what Gaga was trying to tell us. At the time in pop culture, the paparazzi had famously documented Britney Spears shaving her head amid crisis and Lindsay Lohan's losing battle with sobriety. "I wanted to say something about how the celebrity sort of has this inevitable demise that we love to watch," Gaga explained to MTV News. "But are we killing them or are they killing themselves?" When she first explained her vision to network execs over the phone, the line went silent. "Then they said, 'OK, Gaga, we're gonna make it happen,'" she explained. "I just knew I had to bleed to death for four minutes on TV."

THE RED QUEEN

Gaga looked like quite a lady when she met England's Queen Elizabeth II in 2009. Inspired by the monarchs of British history, she wanted to add a modern twist and commissioned the only designer she knew who could tailor latex, Atsuko Kudo, to create an Elizabethan-style red gown with puffed sleeves and a high neck. A team of seven spent two weeks making the garment's dress, underskirts, and sixteenth-century collar, which Gaga also wore to sing "Speechless" for the queen and her family that evening at the annual Royal Variety Performance.

The red latex creation was polarizing, considering Gaga was in the presence of royalty, but Queen Elizabeth seemed amused as she shook hands with the eccentric pop singer, and according to Kudo, it was a watershed moment for her niche industry. "I knew latex had been accepted and that it marked a new step," the London-based designer told Yahoo Style UK.

OFF THE HOOK

Gaga and Beyoncé's music video for "Telephone" is a pop-art visual masterpiece with a *Thelma and Louise*-inspired plot of murder and killer fashion. The ten-minute video starts with Gaga in prison, though the stylish prisoner models not an orange jumpsuit but Chanel, Jean Paul Gaultier, Thierry Mugler, Philip Treacy, and Viktor & Rolf, as well as custom Haus of Gaga accessories like half-smoked cigarette glasses. In another scene, she rolls her hair with Diet Coke cans, a trick she picked up from her mother as a kid.

Once Beyoncé bails Gaga out of jail, the two set off in the Pussy Wagon, the pickup truck driven by Uma Thurman in *Kill Bill*, which director Quentin Tarantino loaned to the pop superstars for "Telephone." They head to a local diner, where Beyoncé slips poison into her jerky boyfriend's coffee. Turns out, Gaga was in the kitchen cooking up deadly meals for everyone else in the restaurant, and once they too keel over, she and Bey dance among the bodies while wearing red, white, and blue ensembles meant to be a commentary on Americana.

"Me and Beyoncé, really, in this video, we wanted there to be a balance between fashion and camp," Gaga told British *Vogue*. "So, we wanted to do a play on the American flag and a play on capitalism. The inspiration for the Americana vibe was that the song 'Telephone' was about being inundated with phone calls. I was playing around, when I wrote that song, with this idea that we were, as a society, becoming more and more obsessed with interacting with each other in a way that was less real. And that led me to this ingesting of capitalism in a way that's not healthy for us. So, it's a commentary on American culture."

MEAT, BUT MAKE IT FASHION

It's the iconic look that launched a thousand Halloween costumes. To accept the award for Video of the Year at the 2010 MTV Video Music Awards, Gaga wore a minidress made entirely of meat, with matching beef clutch and hair accessory. But it wasn't just Lady Gaga hamming it up for attention. It was a statement against the US military's "Don't ask, don't tell" policy that discriminated against nonheterosexual service members. "It's certainly no disrespect to anyone that's vegan or vegetarian," she explained on the *Ellen DeGeneres Show*. "It has many interpretations, but for me this evening it's [saying], 'If we don't stand up for what we believe in, if we don't fight for our rights, pretty soon we're going to have as much rights as the meat on our bones.'"

Gaga didn't fake it either—the dress was made entirely of real meat. Argentinean designer Franc Fernandez went straight to his family butcher to select his fabric, forty pounds of beef. "It smelled like meat," Gaga confirmed in 2021 to *Vogue*. As she recounted, backstage at the VMAs, her stylist Brandon Maxwell had to "sew all of these last bits of meat to me" despite being a vegan.

The perishable garment was preserved by a taxidermist using bleach, formaldehyde, and detergent, and transported in a climate-controlled truck to the Rock and Roll Hall of Fame in Cleveland, where Gaga's meat dress and boots were displayed for years as part of the "Women Who Rock" exhibition. In 2019, the statement piece became the centerpiece of the Haus of Gaga museum inside the Park MGM casino, as part of Mother Monster's Las Vegas residency, Enigma + Jazz & Piano.

DRAG KING

Lady Gaga has taken on countless personas over the years, but one left quite an impression: her male alter ego, Jo Calderone, a tough-talking, cigarette-smoking, beer-swigging, self-described asshole. It started as a "mischievous experiment" with photographer Nick Knight, who shot the pop star in drag for a 2010 men's fashion editorial published in *Vogue Hommes Japan*. As Gaga recounted in *V* magazine, Knight remarked, "Gaga, I believe Jo has to sing." She brought him to life in the "Yoü and I" music video, sitting on Gaga's piano as she plays in a Nebraska cornfield.

Jo stepped into the spotlight weeks later at the 2011 MTV Video Music Awards, where the alter ego walked the red carpet, presented an award to Britney Spears, and performed "Yoü and I" with Queen guitarist Brian May—and never once did Gaga break character. As the crowd at LA's Nokia Theater looked on in confusion, Jo launched into a four-minute tirade against Lady Gaga, whom he claimed was his ex-girlfriend. Pacing the stage in a black blazer with a cigarette in one hand, he complained in his New Jersey accent about her style and personality, and even revealed intimate details about their relationship. Back in the pressroom, Jo fielded questions from reporters and joked about two-timing Gaga with Spears.

LADY GAGA HAS TAKEN ON COUNTLESS PERSONAS OVER THE YEARS, BUT ONE LEFT QUITE AN IMPRESSION: HER MALE ALTER EGO, JO CALDERONE.

Mother Monster must have ended things for good, because we never saw Jo Calderone again.

THE BIRTH OF MOTHER MONSTER

"Born This Way" took on new meaning when Mother Monster arrived at the 2011 Grammy Awards inside a giant egg carried down the red carpet by four men in nude latex. Backstage, she remained "incubating" in the vessel until it was time for her to perform "Born This Way." The egg, which contained an oxygen tank, was then wheeled out onto the darkened stage, and as it opened, Lady Gaga emerged as if newly "born," dressed in nude latex as her second skin.

The singer was so dedicated to the birth concept that she spent seventy-two hours in the womb-like pod, created by high-tech couture designer Hussein Chalayan. During this gestational period, she prepared for the debut performance of "Born This Way" by ruminating on the song's meaning. "The creative vessel was helpful for me to stay focused," Gaga explained on Ryan Seacrest's KIIS-FM radio show. "We had it backstage so that I was able to really stay in this sort of creative, embryonic incubation."

WORLD'S FIRST FLYING DRESS

One small step for pop music, one giant leap for pop culture. Lady Gaga's *Artpop* was a spectacle of experimentation, and not just with her music. At the album's launch party in 2013, she hosted a press conference in a warehouse at the Brooklyn Navy Yard, where she unveiled Volantis, the world's first flying dress. "Do you have any questions or do you want to see her fly?" Gaga asked with a wink. She slipped out of her spacesuit and was strapped into a white carbon fiber dress mold affixed to six lifting rotor units arranged in a hexagonal formation. With the touch of a remote control, the battery-powered Volantis—Latin for "flight"—hovered three feet (1 m) off the ground as it traveled through the air toward reporters. Upon landing safely at the end of the runway, Gaga the artistic astronaut signaled a successful mission to her team with a thumbs-up.

Constructed by TechHaus, the technology branch of the Haus of Gaga, Volantis took two years to complete. But it was just the prototype. Investors were interested in mass-producing the flying dress, explained the singer: "Hopefully, one day you'll own a Volantis of your own." That hasn't happened (at least not yet), but the innovative couture piece did go on display at New York's Intrepid Museum in 2017 as part of the "Drones: Is the Sky the Limit?" exhibition.

LADY STARMAN

Gaga paid tribute to one of her greatest musical inspirations, David Bowie, at the 2016 Grammys—and she dressed the part, recreating several of the late glam rocker's iconic looks. It began on the red carpet with an ode to his Ziggy Stardust era: a fiery red mullet wig and electric-blue satin dress coat custom-made by Marc Jacobs. For her medley of Bowie's greatest hits, she walked onstage in an exact replica of his Kansai Yamamoto kimono-inspired white cape embroidered with traditional Japanese lettering that spelled out "David Bowie." In the 1970s, the "Starman" singer would have stagehands rip away the garment to reveal a secondary look, and on Grammy Night so did Gaga, revealing an embellished white suit and pink boa underneath.

Days before her Bowie ode, Gaga got an everlasting tribute to her idol: a massive tattoo of his *Aladdin Sane* alter ego, a lightning bolt painted across his face and a star over one eye. "This was the image that changed my life," Gaga captioned a Snapchat photo documenting the process.

Serendipitously, she had shared Bowie's impact on her artistry just days before he lost his secret battle with cancer on January 10, 2016. "When I fell in love with David Bowie, when I was living on the Lower East Side, I always felt that his glamor was something he was using to express a message to people that was very healing for their souls," Gaga told the *Hollywood Reporter*. "He is a true, true artist and I don't know if I ever went, 'Oh, I'm going to be that way like this,' or if I arrived upon it slowly, realizing it was my calling and that's what drew me to him."

FASHION EVOLUTION

The theme at the 2019 Met Gala was Camp: Notes on Fashion—and Gaga proved she could write the book with four-looks-in-one that traced the

""TO ME, THIS REALLY LOOKS LIKE AN ELEVATED MODERN PROGRESSION OF WHERE I USED TO BE.""

evolution of her theatrical style in reverse, which "brought it back to the Lower East Side," she revealed to British *Vogue*. "Our version of camp was the old me."

The sixteen-minute choreographed performance shut down the red carpet once Mother Monster made her entrance in a hot pink oversized opera parachute coat with a twenty-five-foot (8 m) train carried by an entourage of five tuxedoed models. In a nod to her *The Fame* era, her blonde wig was adorned with a crown of mini hair bows, mimicking the much larger hair bow from her early years. After four minutes of playing to the cameras, Gaga gestured to designer Brandon Maxwell, who unbuttoned his custom creation to reveal her next act, a black strapless ball gown with an angular bustier and asymmetric silhouette. She feigned modesty as he unzipped the black dress to unveil another hot pink number, a spaghetti-strap column gown. Just then, she had a phone call—an assistant handed Gaga a matte black Judith Leiber clutch shaped like a 1980s brick cellphone that she pretended to chat on as she made the rounds for photographers.

Twelve minutes into the performance art piece, Gaga stripped down to her fourth and final look—a return to the very beginning of her career with a black bra and panty set, covered in Swarovski crystals, with fishnet tights. "To me, this really looks like an elevated modern progression of where I used to be," Gaga told *Vogue*.

PLAYING IT SAFE

Leave it to Lady Gaga to make masks stylish. At the 2020 MTV Video Music Awards, she protected herself from COVID-19 in the most creative fashions, in five different *Chromatica*-themed looks with coordinating face coverings. On the red carpet, she imitated the show's Moon Person trophy in a silver quilted parka and clear helmet by Conrad. "I was wearing face shields before it was a thing," Gaga joked on social media.

Her next appearance at the ceremony was to accept the award for Best Collaboration for "Rain on Me" with Ariana Grande, delivering her speech through what looked like a pink gas mask, made of leather and secured with a buckle over her head, by Cecilio Castrillo. Contrasting the aggressive accessory, she wore a Technicolor Iris van Herpen duchess silk dress, laser-cut to mimic raindrops. Gaga's next look was also a balance of glam and grotesque: a voluminous green taffeta ball gown offset by a steampunk-inspired crimson leather harness mask with studded horns by Lance Victor Moore.

For the Artist of the Year award, Mother Monster looked like she had just arrived from the planet Chromatica in a sequined bodysuit and bespoke Maison Met metal mesh mask that also paired nicely with her fifth and final custom outfit, a chrome ruffled winged train coat by Candice Cuoco.

DOUBLE THREAT

From the start of her music career, Lady Gaga always heard, "You should be an actress." Little did many know, she already was. As a musical theater kid in New York City, she starred in several school productions and studied method acting for a decade at the Lee Strasberg Institute, alma mater of Barbra Streisand, Sally Field, Laura Dern, and Angelina Jolie. "I always wanted to be an actress, much more than I wanted to be a singer," Gaga revealed on *Jimmy Kimmel Live* in 2022 while promoting *House of Gucci*. "But I really was terrible at auditioning."

In college, she tried out for an off-Broadway domestic tour of *Rent*—which she's seen "probably thirty times"—and nearly got the part of Maureen, "but I was too young," she revealed to *Hamilton* creator Lin-Manuel Miranda on *Variety*'s *Actors on Actors* series.

When she pivoted from acting to singing—and channeled her natural talents into cinematic music videos and dramatic stage performances—"record executives told me I was too theater," Gaga told Miranda. Hollywood disagreed, and the offers came pouring in for the pop star, who made cameos on *Gossip Girl* and *The Simpsons* and played an alien in *Men in Black* 3. After the 2011 death of Amy Winehouse, her father publicly stated he wanted Gaga to portray the "Back to Black" singer in a biopic about her turbulent life. The same year, Indian actor Shah Rukh Khan, known as the King of Bollywood, pitched Gaga a starring role in a film opposite him during a one-on-one interview for UTV. "I don't have any illusions of being a lead actress," replied the "Born This Way" singer. "Instead, I would like to be cast in a smaller role."

Just as she hoped, Gaga booked supporting parts in large productions, like Robert Rodriguez's *Machete Kills* (2013) and *Sin City: A Dame to Kill For* (2015), before working her way up to her first starring role in *American Horror Story: Hotel* (2015–2016). To *AHS*'s creator, Ryan Murphy, she's "one of the world's most talented people," as he told *Billboard*. Gaga's character, The Countess, is introduced in a six-minute scene in which she has no dialogue—a sequence that would terrify even the most veteran actor. Before shooting it, "I kept saying to her, 'I know you can do it. You're going to do it. It's going to be great,'" said Murphy. Afterward, he showed her the footage "and she literally wept. She burst into tears. I was worried, but she told me later that it was because she was so happy that somebody believed in her."

"RECORD EXECUTIVES TOLD ME I WAS TOO THEATER."

Emboldened by her Golden Globe–winning performance in *Hotel*, glowing reviews from critics, and record-breaking ratings, the twenty-nine-year-old singer was eager to act more in her thirties—two decades after she first dreamed about making it in Hollywood. "I was a theater kid. I was in jazz band. I went to the Renaissance Faire. I was that girl who got made fun of, that nerdy girl," Gaga recalled to *Billboard*. "I believe in that girl." So do film audiences, who have turned out in droves as she's taken on a romantic musical (*A Star Is Born*), a crime drama (*House of Gucci*), and a psychological thriller (*Joker: Folie à Deux*).

With four Emmy nominations, thirteen Grammy wins, and an Oscar, Gaga is inching closer to EGOT status—and she would "absolutely" do Broadway, which would give her a shot at the "T" for Tony. But she wouldn't necessarily hit the Great White Way as an actress. "I love writing music and I love musical theater . . . So I think I would really enjoy the process of creating a musical," she revealed to *Variety* in 2021. "I've thought about it for a really long time."

MACHETE KILLS
GAGA'S BIG-SCREEN DEBUT

"Rodriguez can claim some credit for providing Lady Gaga with her feature film debut as another iteration of the assassin, but it's not exactly an auspicious start." —*Hollywood Reporter*

DIRECTOR: Robert Rodriguez

CAST: Danny Trejo, Charlie Sheen, Mel Gibson, Michelle Rodriguez, Sofia Vergara, Jessica Alba, Amber Heard, Cuba Gooding Jr., Antonio Banderas

PLOT: In the sequel to 2010's *Machete*, the assassin (Trejo) is recruited by the US president (Sheen) to take out an arms dealer (Gibson) in exchange for American citizenship.

RELEASE DATE: September 19, 2013

BOX OFFICE: $17.5 million

AWARDS: Golden Raspberry for Worst Supporting Actress (Lady Gaga, nominated)

HIT LADY: In the campy action flick, Lady Gaga plays La Chameleón, a vampy hit woman who can drive a vintage van with one hand while firing an assault weapon with the other. The small role was written specifically for the singer, after Robert Rodriguez read she was a fan of the first *Machete*. "I think you're an amazing performer. I bet you probably would be great as an actor," the director told her, and they made a deal to include her in its sequel; if she didn't like her performance, he would cut all her scenes. "She did a fantastic job," Rodriguez raved to *Entertainment Weekly*. "She's really got the star quality."

SNEAK PEEK: Gaga promoted the film to her millions of Little Monsters with an exclusive preview of the *Artpop* track "Aura." Weeks before her highly anticipated album arrived, she dropped a lyric video for the brand-new song featuring scenes from *Machete Kills*.

SCENE-STEALER: Rodriguez was so pleased with Gaga's debut in *Machete Kills* that he cast her in his next film, *Sin City: A Dame to Kill For*. She has only one scene but leaves an impression as Bertha, a diner waitress with a heart of gold, opposite Joseph Gordon-Levitt.

AMERICAN HORROR STORY: HOTEL

THE LADY BECOMES A COUNTESS

"Lady Gaga's American Horror Story performance is her greatest reinvention yet." —TIME

CREATORS: Ryan Murphy, Brad Falchuk

CAST: Sarah Paulson, Evan Peters, Finn Wittrock, Wes Bentley, Matt Bomer, Chloë Sevigny, Cheyenne Jackson, Kathy Bates, Angela Bassett

PLOT: The fifth season of the anthology series checks in at LA's Hotel Cortez, the epicenter of paranormal activity, much of it involving its owner, The Countess (Gaga), a century-old vampire.

RELEASE DATE: October 7, 2015

NETWORK: FX

AWARDS: Golden Globe for Best Actress—Miniseries or Television Film (Lady Gaga); Emmy Awards: eight nominations, including Outstanding Supporting Actress in a Limited Series or Movie (Bates, Paulson)

KILLER QUEEN: To portray The Countess, who sustains herself on the blood of hotel guests, Gaga studied some of the most iconic killers: *Psycho*'s Norman Bates, Hannibal Lecter in *Silence of the Lambs*, even millionaire Robert Durst, the convicted murderer at the center of HBO's *The Jinx*. As she got more into character, she found herself having dark thoughts. "If I'm out at a restaurant or I'm in the car and we're driving past people, I sort of look at them and wonder, 'Gee, I wonder if you're clean. I wonder, if I were to kill you, if it would be worth it for me,'" she told *Variety*.

RECURRING CAST: *Hotel* is the first *AHS* installment without series regular Jessica Lange, but many of the anthology's recurring actors returned, including Sarah Paulson as a resident ghost junkie named Hypodermic Sally, Kathy Bates as hotel manager Iris, and Evan Peters as James Patrick March, the man who built the Hotel Cortez back in 1926 solely as a place for him to murder people.

BLOODBATH: Gaga made quite an impression on her castmates. Ahead of filming, she sent Wes Bentley, who plays a detective investigating a murder at the Cortez, a box of dead flowers and a ripped-up teddy bear. To celebrate the first week of filming, she threw a *Hotel*-themed party at her Los Angeles home—and dyed the pool bloodred. "It was just like an insane *Alice in Wonderland* dream. It was so incredible," Paulson told *EW*.

RATINGS RECORD: An estimated 12.2 million viewers tuned in for the October 7, 2015, premiere, making *Hotel* the most-watched telecast in FX's history.

A STAR IS BORN
ART IMITATES THE SINGER'S RISE

"Gaga, in an ebullient and winningly direct performance, never lets her own star quality get in the way of the character." —*Variety*

DIRECTOR: Bradley Cooper

CAST: Bradley Cooper, Dave Chappelle, Sam Elliott, Andrew Dice Clay

PLOT: A troubled musician (Cooper) falls in love with a young singer (Gaga) and brings her on tour with him, but as her solo career rises, he falls deeper into depression.

RELEASE DATE: October 5, 2018

BOX OFFICE: $436.2 million

AWARDS: Eight Academy Award nominations, including Best Picture, Best Actor (Cooper), and Best Actress (Gaga), and one win for Best Original Song ("Shallow"); five Golden Globe nominations

REEL LIFE: Much of Gaga's character is based on her own rise to fame, and she dug deep into those early memories to portray Ally, particularly how it feels to be anxious onstage. However, in the scene when Ally and Jackson first sing "Shallow" together, Gaga's nerves were the real deal opposite a veteran actor like Cooper. "I was watching him rip, roar on the guitar, and sing. I really felt nervous. I really felt afraid," Gaga recalled to *Entertainment Weekly*. "It really just took me back to that place."

STARS ALIGN: The film is the fourth adaptation of *A Star Is Born*. In the first two, the lead characters are an older actor and a younger actress (played by Janet Gaynor in the 1937 original and Judy Garland in the 1954 remake). The third film, in 1976, changed the story to center around a pair of rock and roll singers, played by Kris Kristofferson and Barbra Streisand—both of whom visited the 2018 set.

AN ARTIST REBORN: *A Star Is Born* had a "transformative" effect on how Gaga views herself as an artist. "There's always a feeling of 'Am I good enough? Am I making something honest? Am I making something true?'" she confessed to *Variety*. "There is a sort of stagnant sadness in me, wondering if I'm enough. Today, I did not see that. I saw something different. I saw a clarity. I saw a truth."

HOUSE OF GUCCI

FASHION KILLS IN THIS BIOPIC

"Lady Gaga's note-perfect performance has a timeless style all its own." —RottenTomatoes.com

DIRECTOR: Ridley Scott

CAST: Jared Leto, Al Pacino, Salma Hayek, Adam Driver

PLOT: Gaga leads an all-star cast as Patrizia Reggiani, who marries into the Gucci dynasty—and then hires hit men to kill her ex-husband, Maurizio (Driver), when he attempts to strip her of the Gucci name.

RELEASE DATE: November 24, 2021

BOX OFFICE: $166.2 million

AWARDS: Screen Actors Guild Award for Outstanding Performance by a Female Actor in a Leading Role (Lady Gaga, nominated)

BAD INFLUENCE: To portray the socialite-turned-convict, Gaga thoroughly researched her character and spent six months working on an Italian accent. However, much to the real Patrizia's chagrin, Gaga didn't meet with her "because I could tell very quickly that this woman wanted to be glorified for this murder," she revealed on ABC's *Good Morning America*. "I didn't want to collude with something I don't believe in . . . she did have her husband murdered."

METHOD TO MADNESS: Gaga leaned into the method acting technique, essentially living as Patrizia for a year and a half, "and I spoke with an accent for nine months of that," she told *Vogue*. "Off camera, [too]. I never broke. I stayed with her." Eventually, Patrizia's darkness took a mental toll on Gaga. "I had a psychiatric nurse with me toward the end of filming," she confessed to *Variety*. "I sort of felt like I had to. I felt that it was safer for me."

OFF-SCRIPT: When the first trailer for *House of Gucci* dropped, Gaga's line, "Father, Son, and the House of Gucci" (said while blessing herself), went viral. Turns out, she ad-libbed it! "I used to do it in my trailer as a prayer before I went to do my scenes," she said on *Jimmy Kimmel Live*. "It just naturally made it in [the film]."

JOKER: FOLIE À DEUX
FALL IN LOVE—AND FALL APART

"We cast Gaga because she's magic." —Todd Phillips to *Entertainment Weekly*

DIRECTOR: Todd Phillips

CAST: Joaquin Phoenix, Catherine Keener, Zazie Beetz, Brendan Gleeson

PLOT: It's no laughing matter when the Joker (Phoenix) falls in love with Harley Quinn (Gaga), a fellow Arkham Asylum inmate in the sequel to the 2019 blockbuster.

RELEASE DATE: October 4, 2024

BUDGET: $200 million

AWARDS: TBD

BAD ROMANCE: Gaga earned her biggest Hollywood paycheck to date—$12 million!—to star opposite Joaquin Phoenix in *Folie à Deux*. The title translates to "madness for two," a reference to the obsessive romance between Arthur Fleck (Phoenix), the Joker, and Harleen Quinzel (Gaga), who adopts the antihero persona Harley Quinn as she falls deeper in love.

JUKEBOX MUSICAL: Unlike the 2019 psychological thriller, the sequel is a musical. When *Joker 2* was announced, *Variety* reported it would feature reinterpretations of at least fifteen "very well-known" songs, including "That's Entertainment" from the 1953 musical *The Band Wagon*, later popularized by Judy Garland.

DOUBLE TROUBLE: Harley Quinn was last portrayed on the big screen by Margot Robbie in 2021's *The Suicide Squad*, but Gaga's character exists in a different DC universe, as the *Joker* franchise is set three decades earlier, in the 1980s. But two Harleys are better than one, Robbie told MTV News. "It makes me so happy because I said from the very beginning that all I want is for Harley Quinn to be one of those characters the way . . . like Macbeth or Batman always gets passed from great actor to great actor . . . It's such an honor to have built a foundation strong enough that Harley can now be one of those characters that other actors get to have a go at playing. And I think [Gaga] will do something incredible with it."

YOUTH & I

A self-described "misfit" growing up, Lady Gaga was bullied for her unique differences—the same attributes that would ultimately make her one of the biggest pop stars on the planet. As she met Little Monsters around the world, she heard similar struggles of self-acceptance and the impact on mental health. Gaga didn't want that dialogue with her fans to end, so in 2012, the singer and her mother, Cynthia Germanotta, cofounded the Born This Way Foundation, built upon the same principles as Gaga's empowering anthem of the same name: bravery, kindness, tolerance, humanity, love, and encouragement of individuality.

"I know it's a big issue because I have twenty million followers on Twitter and the second I put out a song about being yourself and loving who you are, it was pandemonium," Gaga explained on *Oprah's Next Chapter*. "I did it. I hit the nerve . . . I'm not interested in making lukewarm pop music or lukewarm philanthropic efforts."

Much more than a foundation, BTWF is a youth movement and a complete shift in the way people think about bullying. At the launch event, Gaga said she hopes to change "the climate of the school environment" by putting the power in the hands of young people facing these issues, not teachers or the government. She reached her intended audience with her first campaign, the Born Brave Bus, which followed the singer's own Born This Way Tour bus around the US in 2013. The interactive experience engaged fans at each stop, beginning with a preconcert tailgate that welcomed like-minded youth to meet and offered necessary services, like free counseling for people under twenty-five struggling with bullying and depression, as well as games and music.

In 2015, Gaga launched the Emotion Revolution with the Yale Center for Emotional Intelligence and hosted a summit at the university campus in New Haven, Connecticut. Two hundred high schoolers were invited to attend and discuss the importance of emotions in school and life. Gaga led the conversation and got particularly candid about her own struggles with depression, which only worsened with fame. Similarly, she got real about battling anorexia and bulimia as a teenager during BTWF's Body Revolution in 2013.

Recognizing an absence of positive news stories, BTWF launched Channel Kindness, which the organization describes as a platform "to give youth a voice in a media landscape that too often ignores or misrepresents young people." At the launch in 2016, one hundred youth reporters were trained to recognize and broadcast acts of kindness within their own communities. Nearly a decade later, thousands of stories have been shared on ChannelKindness.org, documenting the positive things happening in more than fifty countries around the world.

In 2018, BTWF launched #BeKind21 and invited everyone to practice kindness for twenty-one days—the length of time it typically takes to build a habit—in the month of September, culminating in the United Nations' International Day of Peace. By 2023, the campaign boasted an astounding 291 million pledged acts of kindness, so #BeKind21 expanded into #BeKind365, a digital platform that encourages participants to send uplifting messages via the Gratitude Postal Service. There's also a Kindness Generator that provides hundreds of curated kind acts to incorporate into daily life. In the first year, #BeKind365 inspired more than nineteen million acts of kindness, "underscoring the profound connection between kindness and mental health, as individuals who practice, receive, and witness kindness often exhibit better mental health indicators," reported BTWF.

The foundation also partnered with the National Council for Behavioral Health in 2019 to bring teen Mental Health First Aid training to the US. Structured around the idea that teens first turn to each other for support in times of crisis, the program focused on providing students in grades 10 through 12 in-person training "to learn about mental illnesses, including how to identify and respond to a developing mental health or substance use problem among their peers."

Anyone anywhere can earn BTWF's Be There Certificate after taking a free interactive course (available in multiple languages) designed to enhance mental health literacy in young people, developed by Jack.org in

partnership with BTWF. Participants can learn how to recognize the signs that someone is struggling and understand how to provide support. As of 2023, BTWF reports more than forty thousand people have earned Be There Certificates.

Over the past decade, Born This Way Foundation's guiding force has been Gaga's mother, Cynthia, who regularly hosts panels and speaks at summits, most recently alongside US Surgeon General Vivek Murthy to discuss the loneliness epidemic. As BTWF celebrated its tenth anniversary, she revealed how the work she's put in with Gaga has enriched both of their lives. "One of the greatest gifts that we've ever been given has been the opportunity to sit down with young people across countries and continents and listen to their experiences, struggles, and unwavering hope for their individual—and our collective—futures. It has been fuel for my daughter and me both on our brightest and darkest days and a deep well of inspiration and joy, every day . . . The truth is that the story of Born This Way Foundation did not begin with us and will not end with us either; it is the story of a movement of people that believe in themselves and each other."

MEME QUEEN

When Lady Gaga obsessed over "fame" as an unknown singer in the early aughts, "going viral" wasn't yet a thing. Early in her career, on the verge of Twitter and another decade before TikTok, we LOL'd in real time at her unintentionally hilarious candid moments—which have since been reborn on modern social media. Luckily for those of us who like to doomscroll, Gaga hasn't stopped delivering meme-worthy content.

BUS. CLUB. ANOTHER CLUB. ANOTHER CLUB. PLANE. NEXT PLACE.

How hectic is Lady Gaga's schedule? She laid it out, step by step, in a 2011 interview with *Fuse*. Music journalist Touré asked about the stress of making *Born This Way*, with millions of fans anxiously waiting, versus *The Fame*, when she was unknown and thus could record the album "in peace."

"In peace?!" Gaga exclaimed, her eyes as wide as the brim on her hair-bow hat. "Listen . . ." she started, launching into a two-minute justifiable rant detailing exactly why "peace" was a gross misperception surrounding her debut. Even after "Just Dance" became an international hit, she had to fight for another year "tooth and nail, blood, sweat, and leather, every night, no sleep." Clapping her hands for emphasis, she listed her exhaustive grind: "Bus! Club! Another club! Another club! Plane! Next place! No sleep. No fear. Nobody believed in me."

A decade later, Gaga's interview resurfaced on TikTok, where users employed the audio to describe their own overwhelming lives. The viral quote even made its way to Netflix's *Emily in Paris* in Season 1, when Mindy's friends encourage the failed *Chinese Popstar* contestant to get over her stage fright by chanting, "Plane! Plane! Club! Another club! Another club! Bus! Another club! No sleep! Sing, bitch!"

TALENTED, BRILLIANT, INCREDIBLE, AMAZING . . .

How great is *American Horror Story* creator Ryan Murphy? That was the simple question asked of Gaga by the *Hollywood Reporter* in 2015, as the singer promoted her starring role in the anthology's fifth season, *Hotel*. "Yeah, let me rattle them off," she replied, listing a dozen attributes in just sixteen seconds: "talented, brilliant, incredible, amazing, showstopping, spectacular, never the same, totally unique, completely not ever been done before, unafraid to reference or not reference, put it in a blender, shit on it, vomit on it, eat it, give birth to it . . . he's all those things."

One fan clipped the segment from the interview, and millions of views later, it has become the Internet's favorite meme to offer a compliment when just one word won't suffice. One of the best uses was by singer-songwriter Zara Larsson, who used the Gaga GIF to sum up Mother Monster's epic fashion moment at the 2019 Met Gala.

THERE CAN BE A HUNDRED PEOPLE IN THE ROOM

During the press tour for *A Star Is Born*, Gaga effusively gushed about Bradley Cooper for taking a chance on her as the lead in his film. From red carpets and press conferences to late-night talk shows, the starlet sang his praises—and it was always the same old song, over and over and over again: "There could be a hundred in the room and ninety-nine don't believe in you, but just one does, and that was him." By fan estimations, Gaga uttered the line at least eleven times. There were occasional ad-libs. In an interview with *Entertainment Tonight*, she insisted that the one person in question "can change everything." On *The Graham Norton Show*, the hundred people were "watching" while also being nonbelievers. At an exclusive film screening for Little Monsters in New York City, she observed there were literally a hundred people in the room.

At the 2018 Toronto International Film Festival, Gaga said the line three times: once on the red carpet and twice during the Q&A session. The third instance, she acknowledged, "I probably said this earlier," so she switched up the room capacity to "a thousand people"—and then struggled a bit with crunching the numbers on the fly. Nine hundred and ninety-nine

IS THE PLANET CHROMATICA
PROTECTED BY AN INVISIBLE FORCE FIELD?

people later, she got to the point: "I would not be here without you," she told Cooper. The twelve-time Oscar nominee proved he's a gifted actor because each time Gaga delivered her "one in a hundred" line, Cooper would bow his head in gratitude as if he were hearing the compliment for the first time.

Fan account Gaga Doing Things did the internet a service and made a compilation video—and the hundreds of thousands who engaged with it all believed it was truly a viral moment. At the 2019 Golden Globes, where *A Star Is Born* was nominated for five awards, cohosts Sandra Oh and Andy Samberg praised Gaga's performance during the opening monologue and joked that it proved "there could be a hundred people in the room . . ." The camera cut to the singer in the audience who laughed and yelled out, "It's true!"

I SWITCHED BARISTAS

Gaga artfully dodged an awkward conversation with Caitlyn Jenner at Elton John's Academy Awards viewing party in 2022. The Olympian—who supports a ban on transgender athletes, despite being transgender herself—approached Gaga on the red carpet to say hello and acted like the two were old friends. "Are you spending time around Malibu anymore?" Jenner asked, in a video captured by journalist Bahman Kalbasi. "I haven't seen you at the Starbucks in a while." Gaga, wearing a strapless gown of buttery yellow tulle, gave her the cold shoulder. "I switched baristas," she said, shrugging as she turned away. Three words have never had such power, according to the internet. On X, fan account @GagaDaily reposts the twenty-six-second video every anniversary to its half million followers. Others on social media have declared the IDGAF quip their "excuse for everything." In 2024, when Jenner posted she was "absolutely disgusted" that President Joe Biden declared March 31, Easter Sunday, Transgender Visibility Day, one Little Monster replied, "No wonder she switched baristas."

CHROMATICA BALL INVISIBLE FORCE FIELD

Is the planet Chromatica protected by an invisible force field? On opening night of the Chromatica Ball in Düsseldorf, Germany, a fan video showed Gaga dancing onstage when an object was thrown in her direction—and then intercepted by an unseen power. Within days, the four-second clip garnered over 4.4 million views as online sleuths tried to determine what the heck happened. Among the theories: the "invisible force field" that stopped the projectile (which appeared to be a magazine or notebook) was likely a high-powered fan blowing air away from the stage or a scrim, a lightweight woven fabric widely used for special effects in theatrical productions that can appear transparent when backlit.

ACKNOWLEDGMENTS

A longtime Little Monster-in-training, I used to frequent Gaga's favorite dive bars in New York City, hoping to catch a glimpse of a blond hair bow in the crowd, to no avail. Years later, during the *Artpop* era, I was working on Ryan Seacrest's morning radio show in Los Angeles when she came in to promote "Applause." I was working on my computer right outside the studio door when I felt a presence behind me. I turned around and none other than Lady Gaga—in full "Applause" makeup—was reading over my shoulder! I tried to say hello, but no real sound came out. All these years later, I'm still waiting patiently for that "Telephone" sequel, but until then . . .

Thank you to the many fan archives that do an immeasurable job of keeping track of every fashion moment, performance, award show, magazine cover, interview, music video, tour prop, and on and on, especially Gagapedia and La Maison Gaga.

ABOUT THE AUTHOR

Kathleen Perricone is a freelance writer of long-form magazines (bookazines) with published titles about Marilyn Monroe, John F. Kennedy, Anne Frank, Barack Obama, Taylor Swift, Beyoncé, and dozens more. Over the past two decades, Kathleen has also worked as a celebrity news editor in New York City as well as for Yahoo!, Ryan Seacrest Productions, and for a reality TV family who shall remain nameless. She lives in Los Angeles.

First published in 2025 by Epic Ink, an imprint of The Quarto Group,
142 West 36th Street, 4th Floor, New York, NY 10018, USA
(212) 779-4972 www.Quarto.com

Epic Ink titles are also available at discount for retail, wholesale, promotional, and bulk purchase. For details, contact the Special Sales Manager by email at specialsales@quarto.com or by mail at The Quarto Group, Attn: Special Sales Manager, 100 Cummings Center Suite 265D, Beverly, MA 01915 USA.

10 9 8 7 6 5 4 3 2 1

ISBN: 978-0-7603-9498-4

Digital edition published in 2025
eISBN: 978-0-7603-9499-1

Library of Congress Cataloging-in-Publication Data

Names: Perricone, Kathleen, author.
Title: Lady Gaga is life : a superfan's guide to all things we love about
   Lady Gaga / Kathleen Perricone.
Description: New York : Epic Ink, 2025. | Series: Modern icons ; 5 |
   Summary: "Lady Gaga Is Life is a beautifully illustrated guide that
   explores and celebrates the performer, her music, and her wide-ranging
   career"-- Provided by publisher.
Identifiers: LCCN 2024031078 (print) | LCCN 2024031079 (ebook) | ISBN
   9780760394984 (hardcover) | ISBN 9780760394991 (ebook)
Subjects: LCSH: Lady Gaga. | Lady Gaga--Discography. | Singers--United
   States--Biography. | LCGFT: Biographies. | Discographies.
Classification: LCC ML420.L185 P49 2025 (print) | LCC ML420.L185 (ebook)
   | DDC 782.42164092 [B]--dc23/eng/20240703
LC record available at https://lccn.loc.gov/2024031078
LC ebook record available at https://lccn.loc.gov/2024031079

Group Publisher: Rage Kindelsperger
Senior Acquiring Editor: Nicole James
Creative Director: Laura Drew
Managing Editor: Cara Donaldson
Editor: Katie McGuire
Cover and Interior Design: Beth Middleworth
Book Layout: Danielle Smith-Boldt
Illustrations: Natalia Sanabria

Printed in China